SAFE HAVEN:
THE STORY OF A SHELTER FOR
HOMELESS WOMEN

In this groundbreaking work, urban anthropologist Rae Bridgman explores in careful and intimate detail the perspectives of the women who work and live at Savard's, a unique shelter for homeless women. Bridgman uses the design and development of Savard's – a housing model developed by women for women – as an opportunity to document the project's original vision and what happened once it opened. There are few rules at Savard's. Women may come and go as they wish, and referrals to other services are made only when a woman has indicated interest in taking action on her own behalf. It is a model that aims to provide a safe haven for the chronically homeless.

The study traces the evolution of this type of shelter, providing qualitative research and useful analysis for academics, policy-makers, service providers, and activists. Based on many hours of participant observation as well as interviews and staff records, *Safe Haven* presents a distinct picture of the chronically homeless and those on the frontlines of this lifesaving service.

RAE BRIDGMAN is Associate Dean (Research) and Associate Professor in the Department of City Planning, Faculty of Architecture, University of Manitoba.

For the women who have lived and worked at Savard's

and

For my brother, Ross Anderson

Safe Haven

The Story of a Shelter for Homeless Women

Rae Bridgman

UNIVERSITY OF TORONTO PRESS
Toronto Buffalo London

© University of Toronto Press Incorporated 2003
Toronto Buffalo London
Printed in Canada

ISBN 0-8020-4240-6 (cloth)
ISBN 0-8020-8084-7 (paper)

Printed on acid-free paper

National Library of Canada Cataloguing in Publication

Bridgman, Rae
   Safe Haven : the story of a shelter for homeless women / Rae Bridgman.

   Includes bibliographical references and index.
   ISBN 0-8020-4240-6 (bound).   ISBN 0-8020-8084-7 (pbk.)

   1. Savard's (Toronto, Ont.)   2. Homeless women – Housing –
   Ontario – Toronto.   3. Women's shelters – Ontario – Toronto.   I. Title.

   HV4510.T6B75 2003   362.83′83′09713541   C2003-900155-5

This book has been published with the help of a grant from the Humanities
and Social Sciences Federation of Canada, using funds provided by the
Social Sciences and Humanities Research Council of Canada.

University of Toronto Press acknowledges the financial assistance to its
publishing program of the Canada Council for the Arts and the Ontario
Arts Council.

University of Toronto Press acknowledges the financial support for its
publishing activities of the Government of Canada through the Book
Publishing Industry Development Program (BPIDP).

Contents

Acknowledgments

The greatest thanks must go to the women of Savard's – those who dreamed it, who have nurtured it, and who have lived and worked there. Their stories, ideas, and actions infuse this book. Thanks are due to the Homes First Society for their support of the research. The Homes First Society is a Toronto non-profit charitable corporation dedicated to improving the quality of life for low-income people who have suffered chronic homelessness.

I am also grateful to the University of Toronto Press, particularly Virgil Duff, for editorial suggestions and support.

Gratefully acknowledged is the support of the Social Sciences and Humanities Research Council of Canada (SSHRC) through a Strategic Grant (Women and Change), 1998–2001, and the University of Manitoba Faculty of Architecture.

Notes to the Reader:
The Ethics of Research in a Safe Haven

Permission to use the name of Savard's has been given by the Homes First Society. Pseudonyms or composite portraits have been used to protect the confidentiality of all those who were part of the research for this book. Identifying details have also been changed or excluded in order to protect individuals.

Palpable throughout this research have been ethical issues around access, trust, and confidentiality. At times, during staff meetings or advisory meetings with other front-line workers, I was careful to clarify whether it was appropriate for me to be taking notes. Occasionally, I was told explicitly, 'Please do not take notes.' Control of this part of the research remained with staff members.

The Women Street Survivors Resource Group and Homes First Society were very supportive of the research. They felt it was important for the project to be documented, so others could learn from Savard's example. Their belief was Savard's had the potential to be replicated across national borders and that the documentation process would assist in the study of long-term women's poverty in the context of mental illness. '[The process would] provide ... mechanisms to share this model of urban development, influence public policy related to affordable housing, and advance the rights of this population of historically disadvantaged women across national borders' (Women Street Survivors Group, 1996).

Those who provide shelter and housing for the homeless certainly do not own these people, although they do take on gate-keeping and advocacy roles. Founding ideas about Savard's as a *safe haven*, however, conflicted with interviewing residents or even conducting research about them. Savard's staff saw interviewing as an *intrusive act* contradicting the terms of what a safe haven is or should be.

The conventional action of interviewing, a basic part of so much of the research on homelessness, assumes there is a mutually agreed upon process of asking questions and receiving answers. The research challenges become quite different when someone may not be able to respond to questions or when questions are perceived as invasive and threatening. Novac, Brown, and Gallant (1999:4) have also confronted these difficulties: 'We believe that pooling the observations of those with many years of experience [for example, dedicated front-line workers and service providers] is a particularly effective method for learning about the experiences of long-term homeless women, many of whom are unlikely or unable to answer demanding questions for research purposes.'

Following is an excerpt from previously published work about some of my own early research experiences: '"What are you writing? Why are you writing? I don't want you writing here!" These words were stated directly and angrily. I was actually jotting down a few remind-ers of things I needed to do on the way home. Since that reprimand, I have never again brought out pencil and paper when I was "hanging out" with residents at the housing projects I've been documenting. Writing up the contents of conversations and insights happens after leaving the site, or in a pinch, a visit to the washroom can allow for a few hurried notes' (Bridgman 1999d:113).

One day at Savard's, I heard these words uttered in a rising crescen-do. A staff member at Savard's had just called one of the residents by her name: 'Don't you use my name. Who gave you permission to use my name? It's my name and I don't want you using it!' Even greeting someone may challenge their sense of control.

Ongoing consultation with staff members and sensitivity to the needs of residents were required throughout the research. I was care-ful, over and over again, to explain my presence as a researcher to the women living at Savard's. 'I'm writing a book about Savard's, and the lessons here, for others to learn from them.'

Under the terms of the research relationship with the Homes First Society, I was not allowed to conduct formal interviews with residents, although I had many informal conversations with them. During my research, I was thus able to solicit actively only *some* of Savard's 'Others' to become 'an integral part of the definition of research prob-lems, the representation of historical contexts, and the production and interpretation of texts' (Cole 1992:125). Within such limitations, I have attempted to bring the women's voices, actions, and sense of agency to life throughout this book.

The insights of women living at Savard's could be gathered through informal conversations over a period of months or by sharing a meal or watching a television show together. Heightened ethnographic senses were alert for the non-verbal, the smells, the sounds, the rhythms of coming, staying, and going, the what-was-not-said alongside the what-was-said.

The project's development was affected by the fact that the daily practices of Savard's staff and administrators were under scrutiny, not only internally from within the organization, but also externally. Resource group members and members of a research committee set up to act as a liaison between the Homes First Society and other researchers, who were conducting a small evaluative study of Savard's at the time of my research (Boydell, Gladstone, and Roberts 1999), all contributed to critical reflections on the project's directions. Savard's staff raised a number of concerns, particularly during the period when the other researchers were establishing the parameters of their work. 'Many of the women may not understand fully what the researchers are doing.' 'How can the privacy of the women living at Savard's not be compromised?' 'What about the privacy of staff?' 'The confidentiality of the logs needs to be maintained.' 'How can we gather information in order to persuade funders their money is being well-spent?'

When the project had been open almost a year, I was sitting in the staff office one evening about 10 o'clock. One of the residents came to the door. We had had many casual conversations while watching television together over the previous few months. This night, however, she looked right through me. She spat in her distinct accent: 'You're invisible. I do not see you. You are *invisible.*' Then she turned on her heel and left the doorway. References to 'invisibility' communicated discomfort over being an 'object of study.' Staff members on duty that night commented ruefully, 'The research process is sometimes the same as what we do with the women here. We don't consult them directly. They don't necessarily have a direct say in how we run this place.' In the wee hours of the morning the two staff members began bantering and joking about 'research.' One said to the other, 'You know what a researcher is?' and answered her own question in a whisper, 'A *snoop*! Then she turned to me and said, 'That's what you are. A snoop! You are quiet. You are small. You are watching and listening.' We all began to laugh – was it not true? – and, in this immediate instance, it was not to be resolved.

During an interview, one of Savard's original staff members used the charged word *resistance* in relation to the research component of Savard's: 'Some people are resistant to the idea of having their own work researched, right? There's this sense of not wanting to be observed – like a fishbowl. Or other people are resistant in terms of having the residents researched. A lot of resistance comes from resistance to change, and change is very difficult. It's hard to be an agent of change, but it's also hard to participate in change.'

The story of Savard's was thus shaped in part through the staff's own reflexivity, residents' reflections, and my attendance at development and staff meetings, and presence on-site. I also solicited feedback (from staff members and administrators) on what I was writing about the project, including this book. The boundaries of the research relationship were intimate in a context where they read what we write (Brettell 1996).

The research dynamics contrast with the kind of research Robert Desjarlais (1997) undertook for his book, *Shelter Blues: Sanity and Selfhood among the Homeless*: '[His] relations with the staff remained cordial but distanced, with neither party revealing much to the other' (p. 40). Desjarlais suggests his perspective is 'slanted more to the points of view of [shelter] residents than to those of the staff, and much of what [he knows] is gleaned from everyday conversations' (p. 41). Similarly, however, '[he] spent much of [his] time hanging about, listening to and entering into conversations' (p. 41).

With organizational restructuring, high staff turnover, and funding uncertainties, many of the staff members with whom I worked moved on to other opportunities. This required that my researcher's presence constantly be renegotiated with 'new players.' In some odd way, during the time of my fieldwork, I became a medium of continuity and keeper of the stories.

SAFE HAVEN:
THE STORY OF A SHELTER FOR
HOMELESS WOMEN

CHAPTER ONE

Introduction

> We need to hear their stories because they are telling us something about what dwelling (or home) means today, something about the importance of memory and about the possibility of forging a new vision from/based on the borderlands/frontier experience as a way of life. And they are telling us that this marginal space, this place of unease and discomfort, can be a place of strength, a way forward.
>
> *Sandercock, 'Voices from the Borderlands'*

This book is about women and homelessness. It tells the life history of Savard's, a shelter for chronically homeless women in Toronto. More than four years of fieldwork bring Savard's story to life. The book speaks about the hopes, dreams, and fears of the women I met during the research. These are women who have survived the streets. These are women who have worked for years in the city's shelters and drop-ins. These are women who have worked together to build a safe haven for homeless women.

How did this research begin? What methods were used? What approach did I take? What do I write about? This chapter answers these questions.

Safe Haven: The Story of a Shelter for Homeless Women represents one part of my research on homelessness in Toronto – Canada's largest metropolis, with a population of 2.5 million. I began to document two generations of a pilot housing project (named StreetCity) for seventy homeless women and men in December of 1994.[1] StreetCity was designed to help the 'hardest-to-house' transition from street life to more permanent housing, through a self-governance model. Both

StreetCity (opened in 1988) and the second-generation Strachan House (opened December 1996) were developed by the Homes First Society.[2]

The StreetCity model has been praised as one of Canada's 'best practices for alleviating homelessness' (Canada Mortgage and Housing Corporation 1999a). Levitt Goodman Architects received the Governor General's Award for Excellence in Architecture in 1999 for their design of Strachan House – a renovated nineteenth-century industrial warehouse owned by the City of Toronto. The participation of homeless women and men in the design, development, construction, and operation of StreetCity and Strachan House has drawn international attention.

An advisory resource group and the Homes First Society also developed the Women Street Survivors Project (Savard's, as it came to be known later) in parallel with the plans for Strachan House. The Women Street Survivor Resource Group gathered together women who had worked for many years in shelters and drop-ins for homeless women. Their meetings began in 1993. I was invited to document the project in 1994. The project finally opened in January 1997.[3] Savard's capital costs were funded through the construction budget allocated to Strachan House. It is housed at the easternmost end of that project.[4] Spatially, administratively, and philosophically, however, Savard's maintains quite a distinct identity.

Savard's was named after Diane Savard, who was known to many of Savard's original staff members. She had spent a number of years living on the streets of Toronto, and eventually became a community worker, who in turn was able to help many others come off the streets. Diane Savard died at the age of thirty-seven in 1993.

There are very few rules at Savard's. Weapons, violence, and the use of drugs or alcohol on the premises are not permitted. There are no curfews. Women may come and go as they wish. Women are not required to take medication unless they so choose. Referrals to other services are made only when a woman has indicated interest herself in taking action.

The women do not pay for staying at Savard's. It is funded through the provincial Ministry of Health and municipal per diems (daily set fees). Savard's is staffed twenty-four hours a day, with two staff members on at a time. There is a general policy of no barring or eviction. A resident may, however, be asked to leave temporarily for a period of hours or days, should this be necessary. There is also no specified time limit for length of stay at Savard's, as is generally the case with most other facilities. Women are referred to Savard's by the Hostel Outreach Program (HOP), and a number of social services provide support to complement Savard's mandate.

The women who live at Savard's represent two groups of chronically homeless women: the first comprises middle-aged and older women who have severe mental health problems, usually chronic delusional disorders or depression, which may have worsened over the course of their being homeless. The second group includes younger women with mental health problems that may be undiagnosed. Some of the women are extremely reclusive, distrustful of social service providers or governmental officials. They have been ostracized by society-at-large because of their at times 'bizarre' behaviour (for example, poor hygiene habits, screaming, threatening gestures, self-mutilation). The literature on homelessness tends to define *chronic homelessness* as being without a permanent domicile for at least a year (Brown and Ziefert 1990). Some of the women who come to live at Savard's, however, have lived for more than a decade with chronic homelessness.

Randall Kuhn and Dennis Culhane (1998) have categorized the chronically homeless as an older population with many special needs and health problems (such as physical or mental illnesses or substance abuse problems). Episodically homeless people, who cycle in and out of literal homelessness (that is, living without a roof over their head), are comparatively younger than the chronically homeless, but they also experience significant health problems.

In this book, 'chronically homeless' subsumes the above two descriptions and refers to long-term homelessness (over a period of several years or more) for women who live rough on the streets, or cycle through fleeting periods of being housed (for example, taking a room in a rooming house for a brief period, or staying at a friend's place for several days), using the emergency shelter or hostel system, staying at an institution (for example, jail or a hospital), and living on the streets.[5]

While *Safe Haven* focuses on single chronically homeless women, the term *single* encompasses a wide variety of situations. 'Single may include women who have never been married, young women without children, women whose children are living in foster homes or with other family members, elderly women, heterosexual women, and lesbian women' (Glasser and Bridgman 1999:20). Shelter providers may define a homeless woman as 'single,' but she may not describe herself in this way, and her driving desire may be to reunite with her children.[6] 'An insider's perspective ... may reveal that the woman highly values the role of wife and mother and *does*, in fact, have a partner, *does* have children who visit her in the shelter, and *does* see herself as filling those roles, even if economic factors have placed constraints on her which force her to cycle in and out of the shelter system and leave her unable to care for her children on an ongoing basis' (Lovell [1984] cited in Koegel [1988:11]).

According to the first of Savard's founding First Principles, Savard's was designed for women who 'have fallen through the cracks of social and health services, while others have long histories as survivors of those systems.' Let me mention here two other key First Principles: there were to be no expectations placed on the women to change, and Savard's was to offer a flexible, non-judgmental, low-demand atmosphere and structure. These principles challenge standard practices for many other shelters that rely on limited time periods and regulations around hygiene and acceptable behaviour.

Research Methods

My research on Savard's began in January 1995 and continued until July 2000. Primary research data were gathered through extended participant observation, in keeping with the traditions of anthropological research. Detailed fieldnotes were taken during biweekly design and development meetings for the first two years of the research. Then once the project opened, I attended the staff meetings from January 1997 to June 1998. (These meetings were held weekly until August 1997, at which time the meetings became biweekly.) I also attended the monthly meetings of advisory and resource groups from January 1995 to June 1998.

I was given access to the daily logbooks and minutes of staff meetings, and I attended two day-long focus sessions with staff and resource group members held in January and February 1998. In another day-long session in March 1999, staff revisited Savard's First Principles and related them to current practices. I also conducted follow-up interviews with administrative staff in January and July 2000, May 2002, and February 2003.

An estimated 250 hours of on-site research time was spent observing and participating in the day-to-day rhythms of life at Savard's (particularly during the period January 1997 to June 1998). Bimonthly visits were made from August 1998 to July 1999. Fieldnotes were written up after leaving the site to document informal conversations with residents, administrators, staff working at Savard's, consultants, and other service providers. Unstructured taped interviews (two to four hours in length) with ten of Savard's staff members were conducted, then transcribed. Findings from another study of Savard's conducted by a research team from a local mental health centre (Boydell, Gladstone, and Roberts 1999) also contributed to my own independent study.[7]

The will to undertake such extended research was driven by the idea that it is important to document the *processes* by which a groundbreaking project comes alive. At the heart of this study is the desire to take a keen look at the inherent tensions between the 'vision' (the alternative proposed) and 'practice' (the reality of bringing the vision into being). Such documentation '[can] offer future efforts more concrete guidance in the strengths and weaknesses inherent in various strategies' (Glasser and Bridgman 1999:114). Implementation assessments of demonstration projects generally focus on charting the degree to which the proposed model has been able to be implemented as planned. They look for barriers to implementation and suggest how to address these issues if the project is tried elsewhere. They also identify key (and perhaps unresolved) issues to help guide future research (Mowbray, Cohen, and Bybee 1991:77).

Implementation studies (Sohng 1996; Corbett 2000) are useful for exposing tensions between the preferences and perceptions of 'users,' 'clients,' or 'consumers,' and agency staff, and for exploring organizational, policy, and funding constraints and shifts. E. Fuller Torrey, for instance, did pioneering in work with the mentally ill. His review of four successful community-based initiatives concluded that they were not replicated (or in some instances were disbanded) because of chaotic and confusing funding requirements set by mental health agencies (Torrey 1990). Such findings highlight the potential difficulties of successfully implementing model practices in other contexts. Municipalities and regions have distinct needs, and similar efforts may produce quite different results in other places: best practices may not translate from one context to another. Yet, we are still left with the question why 'each city and each community organization ... [should] have to "reinvent the wheel" when combating homelessness' (Glasser and Bridgman 1999:111).

Many publications present housing 'solutions' to the 'problem.' Typically, we do not learn about how projects have actually come into being. Nor have many researchers explored how projects *evolve over time.* Martha Burt (1992) comments on how many studies of homeless-ness merely *describe* the homeless population. Researchers do not give enough attention to documenting effective interventions for actually alleviating homelessness. Literature on women's homelessness suffers from a lack of research on new and emerging alternative housing projects, to build on the lessons they can offer. There is also room for more documentation and assessment of *housing models developed by women for women* (see Novac, Brown, and Bourbonnais 1996:38; Novac, Brown, and Gallant 1999:59–60). This book intends to redress these imbalances.

I concentrate on the ways in which staff at Savard's, individually and as a group, struggle to fulfil their mandate on a daily basis. How do residents at Savard's challenge the conditions under which shelter is provisionally offered to them? In this 'ethnography of the particular' (Abu-Lughod 1991), grounded attention to the small and the everyday offers insights for understanding larger currents of state responses to homelessness.

Themes

Two uniting themes echo throughout this book: a sense of Savard's contribution to utopianist and feminist critiques of the existing social order; and a commitment to explore multiple ways of communicating ethnography-in-action.

Utopian Pragmatics

Safe Haven documents how an alternative vision is made *real*. The rela-tionship between the alternative proposed (the *vision*) and the reality of living that alternative define the *pragmatics* involved in implementing the proposal (Bridgman 1998b). The focus is on 'bringing "lived life" into closer proximity to our understanding of society and history, and with utilizing this knowledge for the practical amelioration of current social conditions' (Gardiner 1995:90).

James Holston proposes that the 'utopian factor' disrupts 'the imag-ery of what ... society [understands] as the real and the natural ... [and] defamiliarize[s] the normative, moral, aesthetic, and familiar catego-ries of social life.' Holston asks: 'Without a utopian factor are not plans likely to reproduce the oppressive status quo?' He answers his own question: 'Without a utopian factor, plans remain locked in the prison-house of existing conditions' (1989:315–17). Without this utopian factor, dreams of a more just society fade.

With an appreciation of the utopian project – dreaming *a good place that can never be* (this is a rough translation of the Greek in the coined word, utopia) – we can greet Savard's safe haven as one of those 'partial utopias.'[8] It is 'one that we recognize is ragged around the edges, whose boundaries shift and change, and one that requires the vision and knowing of others to patch together the web' (Schneekloth 1994:302).

This research joins other ethnographies focusing on the dynamic between organizations and program participants (for example, Lamphere 1992; Reimer 1997). It joins the lineage of ethnographic research on organizations (for example, Goffman 1961; Foucault 1975; Sachs 1989; Wright 1994). There is also a rich history of ethnographic studies of social service and agency workers (Brookman and Morgen 1988; Erickson 1990; Myers 1997) to which *Safe Haven* contributes.[9]

Three studies, in particular, have directly influenced my ways of approaching analysis of Savard's development. The first, by Nicholas Low and Bruce Crawshaw (1985), analyses the belief systems of those who define problems associated with the homeless, and therefore shape policy. Mark Liddiard and Susan Hutson (1991) have also closely examined how organizations' definitions and processes affect the social construction of homelessness. (Both these articles focus particularly on issues affecting homeless youth.) In a third article, Vincent Lyon-Callo (1998) draws in part on his own 'insider' experiences as a shelter worker and activist. He exposes how the traditional funding sources constrain social actors in the homeless sheltering 'industry.' He critiques, for example, the limits of the federal U.S. Housing and Urban Development (HUD) 'continuum of care' model. This model emphasizes helping homeless people using time-limited case management approaches that 'treat' and 'reform' homeless people (p. 4).

All three articles draw together the insights of those working in the 'shelter industry' and the perspectives of those they seek to help. In a similar vein, this book exposes the multiple and at times conflicting perspectives of homeless women and those working to help them. It also considers the world views of professionals and service providers and how organizational and funding constraints can influence project outcomes.

In *Safe Haven*, the very concept of a safe haven is understood to be a reaction against existing crisis-driven, time-limited, bureaucratic, and rule-bound ways of addressing homelessness. Savard's by its very nature, its very existence, can be understood as a feminist critique of the existing social order. This feminist critique is one that carries inherent tensions, however. One of the staff members first hired to work Savard's mused:

All the staff would probably call themselves feminist. Although we don't talk about it a lot, we acknowledge that women are structurally oppressed – it's complex and it's deep. I think that all of the workers [at Savard's] can make the connections between racial oppression and oppression around sexual preference and disability. Most of those connections are all taken for granted by us. We don't have to hammer any of that out. It's on the table and accepted, which is so refreshing in a workplace. ... In my other workplace, it's really hard even to acknowledge that women are distinctly and differently oppressed. I think that fits in with feminist principles.

When asked about how Savard's was a 'feminist project' during an interview, another staff member spoke about some of the obstacles the Women Street Survivors Project had to face at an organizational level.

There's a whole history to that word [feminist] that is threatening to people who don't think along those lines. Homes First is not a feminist organization, so I don't know how you can really fulfil your mandate as one, if you don't have support from the parent organization, to be that. As a staff person, I feel like a cog in a wheel. I have no control over who else works there, or how they arrive on the scene, or if they're suited to the job, or not suited to the job. We don't have any control in the larger picture, so I don't think that you can really, over the long haul, operate as a feminist organization, if you don't have any influence in the big picture, 'cause that's what it's all about – it's politics, and making change. So, maybe you're making change in a few individual women's lives, but that's just one piece of it.

One of Savard's relief staff interviewed spoke about the perceptions on the part of some Homes First workers that Savard's was being sexist and exclusionary in wanting only women to work at Savard's:

A number of the people who were not happy with Savard's were men who wanted to either work there, or they didn't understand what it was.

They didn't understand why they couldn't work there, because they work with women at other Homes First projects, and they didn't understand what was so different about it at Savard's. Once explained to them, a lot of them understood. But there's a lot of men, I think, in Homes First, that don't understand women's issues. Why women would want a place of their own? Why female staff would want to work with just women? And why they wouldn't want men working with them? These are issues that have never been really talked about in Homes First. And so a lot of them see it as a sexist kind of thing.

A third full-time staff member declared: 'Yes, this is a Homes First project. Yes, we're part of Homes First. But we're *different*. This is a women's project. There are different ways of working here, different needs that need to be accommodated.'

Ethnography in Action

How can ethnographers share the kind of work we do? How can we communicate the patience and endurance required? How can we share the excitement of discoveries made while 'in the field'? These questions also reverberate throughout this book.

Similar questions infused a collaborative exhibition, entitled House/Home (Photo Passage, Harbourfront Centre, Toronto, May–June 1999). The exhibition featured architectural drawings of Strachan House by Levitt Goodman Architects and photographs by Robert Burley and Deborah Friedman of Toronto. Friedman and Burley began photographing the construction of Strachan House in the spring of 1995. Their goal was to create a record of the project from the initial phases of construction through to its inhabited state. Burley documented the architectural components of the project, while Friedman concentrated on making portraits of some of the residents of Strachan House.

The exhibition also included a series of notebook entries from fieldnotes, entitled *Journeys Home: Fragments from Fieldnotes, Strachan House, 1997–1998*. The fieldnotes in the exhibition were not fieldnotes in the truest sense, for they were at one (further and refined) remove from my original fieldnotes – those records of the mundane, the quotidian, the inchoate, the (at times) barely understood, at the time they were written. The notes had to be written so others could read them. A conscious decision was made to print by hand to retain a sense of the immediacy with which the original notes had been written (Bridgman 1999a, 2002a).

Inspired by the House/Home exhibition, *Safe Haven* captures what happens when we do fieldwork and analyse our notes. The book includes passages from fieldnotes, excerpts from transcriptions of meetings and interviews, ethnographic moments crystallized in poetic fragments, and simulated logbook entries – all conjoined with linear prose.

There are others who have experimented with ethnographic representation. Margery Wolf's book, *A Thrice-Told Tale: Feminism, Postmodernism, and Ethnographic Responsibility* (1992), for instance, pushes us to think about how ethnographic insights can be shared through other than conventional academic prose. In *A Thrice-Told Tale*, Wolf uses three different texts generated from her fieldwork in Taiwan. She writes a fictional story based on her fieldwork, includes excerpts from fieldnotes, and reprints one of her articles published in the *American Ethnologist*. The texts all focus on one particular event in the village where she was living. Each shifts perspective. Each is written in a different style. Each tells the 'story' differently.

This book's writing strategies try to impart a sense of what it is like to undertake long-term fieldwork. What a fragmentary and painstaking process it is to witness and to 'hang out' (Rosenthal 1991). *Safe Haven* explores the convergence of the languages associated with social science, literature, and other modes of writing. It partakes of a

> discourse where the beauty
> and the tragedy of the world
> are textually empowered
> by the carefully chosen constructions
> and subjective understandings of the author
> (Benson 1993:xi).

Safe Haven contributes to the ever-growing body of literature on feminist theory and practice in anthropology. It follows in spirit from recent Canadian work, particularly *Feminist Fields: Ethnographic Insights* (Bridgman, Cole, and Howard-Bobiwash 1999) and *Ethnographic Feminisms: Essays in Anthropology* (Cole and Phillips 1995).

Safe Haven thus reflects on the relationships among the researched and the researcher and the profound effects they have on each other. Feminist practitioners generally acknowledge complex differences in relative power between people. They try to give voice in multiple (and often experimental) ways to those they represent. They have an ongoing interest in bringing forth 'submerged perspectives' through their ethnographic research. They are also keen to explore the transformative potential of women's work. (See Bridgman, Cole, and Howard-Bobiwash 1999:3.) These principles underlie this book.

This introductory chapter outlines how and why the research began and what methods and approaches were used. It also provides an overview of the themes that saturate the book. The second chapter, 'Reach Out,' draws directly on some of my fieldnotes, to share what it is like to do street outreach with homeless women in Toronto. Chapter 3, 'Shelter Women,' begins with three questions. Why are there homeless women? Why can we not help all the homeless women? Why do we need a Savard's? This chapter describes conditions under which homeless women live. It also surveys some of the existing facilities designed to alleviate women's poverty and homelessness. Chapter 3 provides a larger context for the life history of one small shelter.

The subsequent chapters unfold in chronological fashion. Chapter 4, 'Safe Haven,' charts how the Women Street Survivors Project started as an alternative to existing paradigms. What is a safe haven? Ideas about non-intervention and zero eviction were the subject of many early planning discussions. Chapter 5, 'By Design,' focuses on the design phase of the project and staff hiring. What ideals drove the design ideas and program plans? Who would come to work at Savard's? What questions were asked of those applying to work there? These questions circled around the most basic of all questions – how could the project answer the needs of women street survivors? Boundaries permeate: between privacy and publicness, inside and outside, safety and danger, structure and flexibility, trust and dependency. Chapter 6, 'Come Inside,' documents moments of inhabitation at Savard's. Small everyday acts can speak volumes about large issues. The chapter simulates a series of logbook entries written by staff at Savard's. Chapter 7, 'Natural Progression,' looks at changes during the first three years of Savard's operation. How did ideas about non-intervention play out? How did the project change over time? The last chapter, 'Long Road from the Street,' offers a summary of the concrete lessons Savard's offers.

Safe Haven is written for those who want to learn more about the work being done to help homeless women – who live in our very midst. The hope is that Savard's will inspire other initiatives to help women street survivors.

There is a growing and rich literature on the gathering of life histories – the life histories of individuals. While many narratives of the homeless have been gathered and published, there is the danger of sensationalizing their experiences and profiting from someone else's pain. The legions of government officials, social service providers, journalists, researchers, and others stoke the fires of an 'industry' that earns them the name 'poverty pimps.' The baseline question for any research on homelessness must be, How does the research challenge the very conditions it describes?

For all these reasons, this book does not attempt to tell the stories of abuse, neglect, sorrows, and joys of the women who have come to live at Savard's, although several of the women did tell me their stories.[10] Nor does it tell the life stories of all those who have worked there.

During the main period of my research (1995 to 1999), Savard's went through a number of phases:

> *Phase 1* (January 1995 to December 1996). The vision. Planning the Women Street Survivors Project.
>
> *Phase 2* (January – December 1997). The first year. The Women Street Survivors Project opens, with beds for ten women. The first resident moves in 15 January. Shortly after opening, it is renamed Savard's by staff.
>
> *Phase 3* (January – December 1998). The second year. A new generation of staff has been hired. By the end of 1998, most of the original full-time staffing group have left. There are major administrative and organizational changes in the Homes First Society.
>
> *Phase 4* (January – December 1999). The third year. With funding constraints, the number of women living at Savard's increases from ten to a maximum of fifteen. (Thirteen beds are for residents, and two are designated for drop-in or emergency use.) Savard's original designation as a 'pilot project' ends in May 1999. Permanent core funding is allocated by the Ontario Ministry of Health. The last one of the original full-time staff has departed.

Through telling the life history of the safe haven, the venture takes on a life of its own – beyond the stories of any one person who has lived and worked there. In the words of Regna Darnell (1999:29), 'There is a culture of the shelter and a society of its inhabitants at any given moment; these are storied, producing in sum a larger story of place and person.' Savard's 'exists' through the actions of those who have helped to build it and those who live and work there. Its history is traced through the archival minutes of meetings, the lived experiences of those who pass through its doors, and the stories that people tell about it. The physical site of Savard's also *speaks* about how homeless women make space their own. Savard's story is complex and multidimensional. This chapter began with an admonition from Leonie Sandercock, 'We need to hear their stories.' Savard's story is one that tells us about home, homelessness, new visions, places of strength, and a way forward.

CHAPTER TWO

Reach Out

Emerald Green
She walks into the City shelter.
Her bags are searched for weapons.
'Any knives, mace, spray oven cleaner?'
'No.'
Maggots indescribable.
One pork chop
rock-hard crystallized emerald green.
'Do you need this?'
'Yes.'

Saran Wrap
Oozing skin saran-veiled
but for eyes
and mouth.
Everything in the purse
swaddled in Saran Wrap
each penny encased.

Night Flight
All her fingers are lost
her thumbs remain.
'She won't eat anything we've made –
she'll eat that can of peas.
But don't you go tryin' to open it for her.
She won't stay long.'

Purse
Wrinkled pink telephone message memo
    (*Can you come to Fran's and meet me there?*)
pizza pamphlet
2 condoms
4 pennies
1 turquoise blue earring
1 silver drop earring
1 package Marlboro Lights cigarettes
Welcome to the Scott Mission pamphlet
1 plastic Superhero
Shopper's Drug Mart prescription
1 rotten apple
all spill on the sidewalk.

The Garden
Little sticks
mark each spot.
Into freshly turned earth
she transplants
seven ragweed plants
neatly spaced
in a row.

Acetone Rituals
Swollen hands apply
black magic marker
to eyes.
Trembling slate green
polish thickens
reds and pinks
of nail enamel.

Acts of Care
She shits on the street.
She does not want to
use the toilet.
This pollutes Lake Ontario.
Later she waters

curdled plants
with milk –
an act of care
that kills.

The fragments beginning this chapter are drawn from my fieldnotes. They are inspired by anecdotes from front-line workers about long-term homeless women they have known or moments witnessed during my fieldwork.

What is it like to do street outreach with chronically homeless women? Chapter 2 answers this question. Outreach to the most marginalized women living on the streets of Toronto – the Resource Group identified this as essential, in order for Savard's to accommodate these women. The need for long-term, intensive, and flexible outreach to homeless people living on the street was recognized in the 1996 report, *Metropolitan Toronto Mental Health Reform* (Metropolitan Toronto District Health Council 1996). As well, this report recognized 'the lengthy process necessary to build trust with the service provider' (p. 29).

Outreach to women living on the street began three months before Savard's opened. The expertise of the Hostel Outreach Program (HOP) was used, as they had already established links with women who were using the shelter system sporadically or were living on the street.

Following are excerpts from fieldnotes, dated 15 May 1997, 3:00 pm to 10:00 pm. I walked with two outreach workers. They were doing their rounds in the downtown area (from Yonge Street to Bay Street, bounded to the north by the Eaton's Centre and to the south by Union Station). I wrote up fieldnotes after returning home that night.

At that time, the outreach workers had identified about sixty seriously mentally ill women living in and around City Hall and Union Station.

I meet Mary and Charlotte at New City Hall. We're supposed to meet by the big pool, but end up missing each other. We are at opposite ends of the pool, of course! It is a rainy afternoon. Grey skies and a cold brisk wind. Mary and Charlotte are both dressed casually in blue jeans and jackets. We aren't able to see anyone who usually hangs out at City Hall. We stroll over to the Eaton's Centre.

Mary's and Charlotte's eyes are roving. They're always scanning for women they already know. Or women they have not made contact with yet. Scanning is really the right word. Every 'sixth sense' is taut, stretched, alert.

We walk slowly up Yonge Street from Queen, along the east side of the Eaton's Centre. Then we spot a woman lurking in one of the bays of the Eaton's Centre. She is standing with her hands in her pockets. Dark sunglasses cover her eyes. A black knit scarf covers her head and face, so that only the glasses are visible. She wears dark clothes. She carries a handbag and one plastic bag with her. Nothing of her skin is visible, but for her nose. She appears to be a black woman. Mary has seen her before and noticed that underneath the black scarf, a plastic bag was wrapped around her hair.

This night, Mary tries to approach to introduce herself, but the woman moves away quickly. I am standing quite far back behind one of the large columns. The woman seems very nervous and definitely does not want to be approached. Mary tries again to make contact, but the woman evades her and walks quickly away. Mary comes back to Charlotte and me. She is shaking her head and comments that the woman seems scared and unusually 'skittish.' 'We may see her again.' They will try to make contact if they have another opportunity. Perhaps they will put some money down on the sidewalk. She can choose to pick it up, if she wishes.

At the corner of Dundas and Yonge, there is another woman. She is very thin. She sits on the cold concrete bench, with her bare legs crossed. An off-white canvas hat is pulled down low over her brow. She is wearing a very light jacket. Mary says someone had told them about this woman, but this is the first time they have seen her. Mary mentions that she thought the police would tip them off about women more, but just 'ordinary citizens' have been the most helpful.

The woman is slight and looks wan and distracted. Mary and Charlotte spotted her before I did. Mary goes and sits down beside her, while Charlotte and I wander off, so that Mary and Charlotte will not be perceived as being together. Charlotte tells me that they often separate when they are trying to make contact with a woman. If one is unsuccessful in communicating, the second can try again – without being associated with the first.

I watch covertly from a distance. Mary offers the woman a cigarette which she accepts. The Eaton's Centre is a mecca for so many – some sitting, some standing, some loitering and milling about. Charlotte talks to the man selling sunglasses in a small booth on the sidewalk to see if he has seen Lily. He has worked in the past with homeless people, apparently, and has been a good source of information for them. They are on the lookout for Lily and ask a couple of the other vendors (they confer with them on a regular basis) to see if they have seen Lily. No one has.

I catch sight of April with her matched blue luggage carried on a stand with wheels. She's wearing a blue coat and hurries into the Eaton Centre at the far end from where we are standing. Charlotte bumped into April outside earlier, but she did not want to talk with Charlotte. Charlotte remarks, 'She's on a mission.'

Charlotte has gone to get some warmer clothing for the woman they have just made contact with at the corner. The car is parked a few blocks away. It holds clothing and some food supplies. Mary slips the woman some money (they carry money with them – a maximum of $10 per person). By the time Charlotte gets back twenty minutes later, though, the woman has already taken off.

We decide to head south back down Yonge Street. All of a sudden, from what seems like nowhere, a woman walks by us. Quickly, so quickly, with fast small steps. She is wearing tattered sneakers and a torn T-shirt. The shirt could have been white at one point. Wrapped around her bottom half is something that looks like it may be a long-sleeved T-shirt, of the same indeterminate shade of dirt-white. She looks distressed and is holding her arms folded in front of her. Her body is caved in, her hair dishevelled – she mumbles to herself as she foots past us.

Mary says sharply – 'Lily.' 'Lily' stops for a moment, a moment long enough for Mary and Charlotte to ask her if she would like some leggings (they are the colour of green marshmallows). Lily utters some sounds, indistinguishable consonants and vowels, but she takes the proffered leggings and scoots off with them, even as they are trying to give her a warm vest. Charlotte says to Mary, 'Here, she can take my jacket.' Lily, though, is long gone, heading south at a clip that is hard to keep up with. She disappears. We try to follow but quickly lose her. Then we catch sight of a figure wearing the tights, still speeding along Yonge Street. Lily is under five feet tall, and looks Asian. We lose her again, and Mary and Charlotte decide to split up to look for her. Charlotte heads down into the subway.

I go with Mary. I am thinking, how impossible this is, to find someone who does not want to be found, amidst such crowds of people. Mary tells me that it took a while for both Charlotte and herself to find out where people like to hang out, what their haunts are, what their routes are. They have been doing outreach for several months now, and it is distressing that their contracts are due to end 6 June, when they have really just begun to make contact with some of the women. We round the corner of the Eaton's Centre on Queen Street, and Lily is right there before us. She is talking to a couple of well-dressed people who cross the street when the light changes. Charlotte waits, then speaks to her, and tries to suggest that Lily come with her for some Chinese food. Lily seems interested, but then suddenly disappears again. She has run down the subway stairs and is gone. Lily is wearing nothing but the clothes I have described, and carries nothing with her. She is incoherent and speaks but seeming gibberish, with words occasionally flashing in that 'make sense.'

Mary tells me that they are going to try to 'form' her the following morning – have her certified and committed for psychiatric assessment. ('Form,' 'certified,' and 'committed' carry loads of metaphoric weight.)

Mary is concerned that if she does go in to the hospital, they will only keep her three days. It is a long weekend, and if Lily wants to leave, Mary will not be able to follow up, and the hospital may release her back to the street. We have a discussion about how they will find Lily in the morning. She often goes to McDonald's in the early morning, but has been asked to leave because she has been eating all the ketchup. Mary and Charlotte have seen her eating food from the garbage. They talk about how they will coordinate with Dr Tomlinson so that he can form her. They'll use their cell phones, in case one of them has to tail or chase Lily.

Mary and I head back up Yonge Street to the corner of Dundas to see if we can catch sight of the woman with the hat. On the way, the black woman with her head and face all covered is standing in one of the Eaton Centre's bays again. Mary tries to approach – but to the same effect – unsuccessful. The evening continues on, with the same sense in my mind of seek-and-chase, looking for the 'wild goose.' We check spots where someone is known to come: the washrooms at City Hall, the Bus Terminal, the washrooms at Union Station, the bottom level of Union Station where departures for the GO trains are, a particular grate on a particular corner. Mary takes me to the spot where 'Hannah's grate' is, but there is no sign of Hannah. Mary also confers with the security guards at Union Station. One of them phoned her two nights ago with a lead about a woman.

It transforms the city to think of the great furnace of heating pipes beneath the hallways and corridors of the street, where someone can 'claim' a grate (a 'hearth') to survive. I think of Anne Lovell's 'The City Is My Mother.' The air from the grates does not feel at all warm tonight. Later, Charlotte tells Mary that 'Hannah's grate' actually moved from that spot, to the grate across the street on the north corner.

At the bus station, Mary and I stop to chat with a YWCA First-Stop Community Welcome counter. They are there to help people when they first get off the bus to Toronto and to help people in crisis. The two young women behind the counter tell us about the time a woman got off the bus with her three young children. The mother told them her husband had just died, and she had bought bus tickets and brought her kids to Toronto. The children were bewildered, and the woman seemed to be in state of shock.

Mary confers with the Community Welcome women about whether they have seen the 'woman with the rabbit.' They have not. Mary also tells me later the story of another woman who carried a chinchilla about with her. She had purchased the chinchilla, and managed to take care of it for a while, while living on the street. Then the chinchilla had died, and the woman had cut off its head by mistake. In mourning, she carried the head and the body with her for months thereafter. This same woman had also carried a mouse under her shirt; she had wrapped her torso in tape so that she would be able to clean herself easily, if the mouse peed. These are stories of the ordinary, stories of the understandable – if you suspend your own frames of logic for an instant.

8:30 pm: One of the tall, tall bank towers, beneath this citadel of wealth – Mary and I check there to catch those who are preparing for their night's slumber. One man is sleeping on a length of cardboard over a grate, his bike at his feet, no blanket. He seems to have no possessions aside from the bicycle. Another has set up a more elaborate version of shelter with a box and a sleeping bag. On top of his box he has carefully laid out a brown towel and what appear to be a few ordered toiletries. Everyone takes off their shoes to go to sleep and puts them under their head.

Another man is already asleep in his cardboard shelter. Near him, an Aboriginal man has gone to sleep with no blanket. His buddy is attempting to pull him into a box. The Aboriginal man is roused with great difficulty and curses his chum for disturbing him. He is barely able to speak, but the older Caucasian man seems to be taking care of him, and tries to give him the clean pair of socks that Mary offers. The

Native man's socks are wet. Mary says to me afterward, she wonders if the Native man was not doing solvents, because of his disorientation, his shaking, and the slight film of white powder over his hands. (I had not noticed the white film on his hands.)

Close by, Tanya is uttering animal sounds. This is the woman whom I have heard about during Savard's staff meetings. I do not have an opportunity actually to see her. She is in the southernmost shelter of the grate parade within the most elaborate of the cardboard box constructions, underneath blue plastic strung up with rope. There is also an umbrella and a garden chair. I cannot see Tanya – only the man with her. As we leave, I hear a loud high-pitched scream from within a tumble of blankets – Tanya.

We walk back to the Eaton Centre and there we meet Melinda sitting in the food court. Mary and Charlotte have been encouraging Melinda to consider Savard's for a couple of months now. We first meet Melinda in the early evening, and then we return three hours later. She is sitting in the same spot still. She tells us that she tried to go outside, but it was raining too hard.

Melinda is a Filipina, and has been living on the streets for at least three years. Her two pieces of luggage are strapped to a carrier on wheels. She wears a winter jacket, forest green, with green fur around the hood. She wears sparkling earrings, and her hair is carefully gathered to the back with a clip. A necklace around her neck completes a picture of perfect appointment. She is gracious. Mary and Charlotte mention Savard's to her several times, but she only smiles. Eventually she does take a card from them with the address, and asks, 'Are the women [at Savard's] "normals"?' She tells us that she never stays at a hostel. She sleeps at City Hall on one of the benches by the pool.

All four of us sit at the table of the food court and chat for an hour or more about Melinda's journal-writing, the 'research' she is doing (as she calls it), news about some of her friends in the United States, her studies in the Philippines in psychology, and her nursing. She unpacks one of her bags to show me a number of coil-bound journals (her research journals), but does not open them. She came to Canada twenty years ago as a nanny and has three grown children living here (a son and two daughters). On one level, Melinda is able to hold a gracious conversation. Her manner is gentle and genteel. But the conversation strays into the improbable at times, and things do not always seem to make sense.

At one point, we witness a bit of commotion at another table in the food court. An older woman, short and white-haired, with a very, very swollen right ankle, seems to be harassing a couple of young mothers sitting with their four children. At first, they try to ignore her, but eventually security is summoned. The woman is foul-mouthed and utters obscenities to herself and others. Mary tries to make contact with the woman before security arrives, but the woman does not acknowledge her presence. Mary tries to intervene again when the woman is being escorted out by the uniformed security man. He speaks into his walkie-talkie, as he accompanies the woman out. The woman hurls more obscenities. Mary returns to our table.

Melinda purses her lips and shakes her head as she watches all this. A few minutes later, we bid goodnight to Melinda, and call it a night ourselves. Mary leaves some money with Melinda, who first declines, but then accepts it with thanks after Mary reassures her.

CHAPTER THREE

Shelter Women

Why are there homeless women? Why can we not help all the homeless women? Why do we need Savard's?

The title for the third chapter carries a certain ambiguity. The choice is deliberate, for it draws attention to two vantage points: one focuses on chronically homeless women, themselves, and the conditions under which they live their lives. The other considers the perspectives of those who would help their homeless sisters and have tried to give them solace and shelter. For there are many approaches to providing shelter and support for homeless women.

'Shelter Women' synthesizes themes from the literature on homelessness in Canada, conceptualizes contemporary homelessness, describes the lives of homeless women, and surveys briefly some of the existing facilities designed to alleviate women's homelessness. Chapter 3 provides a larger context for the story of one small project. It answers the question: How have homeless women's needs been translated into action that alleviates their homelessness?

Defining Homelessness and Counting the Homeless

The now voluminous literature on homelessness in North America devotes much attention both to *defining* homelessness and then *counting* the homeless with classificatory rigour. Definitions shift in relation to concepts of adequacy and affordability, visibility and invisibility, problems with statistical data collection with a transient population, and bias in the majority of studies that rely on one-point-in-time interviews with the homeless. Who is or is not homeless remains a slippery question. An introductory caveat in one report states: '[Homelessness] is a confusing term due to conceptual imprecision, fuzzy boundaries, influence of political agendas, the heterogeneity of the homeless population, and the assumptions and attitude of the housed population' (British Columbia Ministry of Social Development and Economic Security 2001).

Peter Rossi and colleagues distinguish between the literally homeless (who obviously have no access to any sort of conventional dwelling place, and live out their private lives in public spaces) and the precariously housed (who may be doubled up temporarily with friends or family or live in pay-by-the-week accommodation) (1987: 1336). Most anthropologists try to privilege whether a homeless person self-identifies as homeless. The self-appellation of the homeless themselves, however, is also fraught with problems.

Sophie Watson and Helen Austerberry (1986 were among the very first to undertake a comprehensive feminist analysis of homeless women's perspectives on homelessness, through collecting the housing histories of homeless women in Great Britain. Importantly, they analysed social policies that privileged nuclear families within market-dominated housing systems and accounted for single women's vulnerability to homelessness.[1] During their study they asked homeless women, 'Do you think of yourself as being homeless?' 'What does the word *homeless* mean to you?' Thirty per cent of the women did not think of where they were then living as home. But neither did they think of themselves as homeless. Another 32 per cent, who did consider their present accommodation as home, also referred to themselves as homeless.

In this book (and following the definition in Chapter 1), chronically homeless is used to describe women who live rough on the streets, or cycle through fleeting periods of being housed (for example, living in a rooming house for a brief period or staying at a friend's place for several days), using the emergency hostel system, staying at an institution (for example, jail or hospital), and living on the streets.

From *A Profile of the Toronto Homeless Population* (Springer, Mars, and Dennison 1998), a report collating nine years of administrative data on hostel use in Toronto (1988–96), a total of 170,000 different individuals (or 133,000 households) stayed at least one night in the Toronto hostel system. Of these, about 17 per cent stayed for one year or more (in total, not necessarily consecutively). Another 9 per cent had been in the system for one to three years, 5 per cent for three to six years, and 3 per cent for more than six years. In 1996 alone, more than 26,000 individuals used Toronto hostels. Of those, 4,300 were considered long-term users. There are significant numbers of people using the hostel system as a form of 'permanent housing.'

Women on the Rough Edge: A Decade of Change for Long-Term Homeless Women (Novac, Brown, and Gallant 1999), building on the Springer report above, surveys the changing patterns for long-term homeless women – specifically in the Toronto area over the past ten years. The proportion of women using the emergency shelter system in Toronto increased steadily from 24 to 37 per cent between 1988 and 1996 (p. vii). From 1993 to 1996, spousal abuse (cited as a reason for admittance to hostels) rose from 6.5 per cent to 10 per cent (Springer, Mars, and Dennison 1998:31). The most vulnerable women, many of whom carry traumatic histories of abuse, are staying homeless for longer periods. A large number of these women have severe physical and mental health problems and multiple needs that entail costly emergency services.

The Novac report also highlights the fact that Aboriginal people (estimates ranged from 5 to 15 per cent) and black people (estimated at 15 per cent) also appeared to be overrepresented among the homeless. This is confirmed in another 1998 report by the Mental Health Policy Research Group (1998).[2]

David Hulchanski, co-author of a study for the Canadian federal government on estimating homelessness (Peressini, McDonald, and Hulchanski 1996), asks wisely in one commentary: 'How many homeless people are there? In Toronto? In Canada? Who knows? No one knows. For some, it seems, trying to count them is more important than taking action.' He ends his commentary with, 'We already know more than enough about the nature and magnitude of the problem to embark on rehousing and prevention programs. Addressing "homelessness" is a political problem, not a statistical or definitional problem' (Hulchanski 2000).

Homeless in Toronto

Women's homelessness, and therefore the very life history of Savard's, have unfolded amidst a tale of Canadian federal and provincial governments' growing reluctance to continue subsidized social housing programs and their reluctance to help those who are unable to obtain housing on the open 'free' market. The result has been to pass responsibility for social housing needs increasingly to the municipal level with devastating results. Amidst the feast of federal devolution, provincial downloading, cancellation of social housing construction (the federal government ended funding for new non-profit housing development in 1993, and the government of Ontario ended funding in 1995), sales of social housing, welfare cuts, rent control changes, and evictions, the numbers of homeless swell.[3]

They swell, witnessed by growing media coverage in Canada on homelessness, numerous government reports (see note 2 in this chapter) and the publication of several books (see, for example, Daly 1996; Layton 2000; O'Reilly-Fleming 1993). The United Nations conducted its formal five-year review and evaluation of Canada's compliance with basic human rights in 1999. In its report, the U.N. Human Rights Committee (1999) was highly critical with regard to many domestic human rights – including violations against Aboriginal peoples and refugees; violations of the privacy rights of people on social assistance; Ontario's act to prevent unionization of workfare recipients; children's rights and benefits; and a disproportionate number of women in poverty. Explicitly highlighted were serious health problems and deaths on the street due to homelessness.

Crisis-oriented emergency and temporary 'solutions' to the 'problem' are increasingly being embraced, causing researchers in one report to observe: 'Some politicians and members of the public seem to be primarily concerned about risks to business development ... and law enforcement mechanisms have been adopted and reinstituted to eliminate visible signs of homelessness and destitution ... The rallying cries of the "Housing Not Hostels" campaign has become a hoarse whisper among those closely involved in working with the poor ... "It's not just bandaid solutions, it's dirty bandaids now"' (Novac, Brown, and Gallant 1999:24).

In a State of Emergency Declaration issued 8 October 1998, homelessness was declared a national disaster in Canada by the activist group Toronto Disaster Relief Committee. An urgent call for emergency humanitarian relief and prevention measures was issued. That same month, Toronto City Council passed the following motion: 'That the Provincial and Federal Governments be requested to declare homelessness a national disaster requiring emergency humanitarian relief and be urged to immediately develop and implement a National Homelessness Relief and Prevention Strategy using disaster relief funds, both to provide the homeless with immediate health protection and housing and to prevent further homelessness (Minutes of the Meeting of Toronto City Council, 28 October 1998).

With the appointment of Claudette Bradshaw to coordinate the federal response to homelessness in 1999 and her subsequent across-Canada research tour, $753 million in funding over a three-year period was pledged to address homelessness issues. Approximately half the money was given over to expanding the existing Residential Rehabilitation Assistance Program. Other funds went primarily to community-based shelter initiatives and Aboriginal projects. The funds could not be used for affordable housing, however. This was made quite explicit. Claudette Bradshaw stated repeatedly that she was not the Minister of Housing (see Layton 2000:188–9). There is still no national housing policy in place in Canada.

Homelessness and Mental Illness

A large part of the general literature on homelessness has focused on mental illness as an important risk factor. Whether mental illness is a cause or consequence of homelessness continues to be an ongoing debate. Symptoms of mental illness (talking to oneself, pacing, screaming, rummaging through garbage), however, can often scarcely be distinguished from adaptive survival strategies (Glasser and Bridgman 1999:67–78).

The rates of mental illness among the homeless population have, however, been of great interest to researchers and the general public. U.S. reports have concluded that 20 to 50 per cent of the homeless suffer from severe mental illness (for example, paranoia, personality disorders, bipolar disease), in comparison to 1 per cent in the general population (Burt 1992:108–9; see also Glasser and Bridgman 1999:25). Toronto studies suggest that at least 30 per cent (or almost 7,000 individuals) of an estimated 20,000 homeless have serious mental health problems (Metropolitan District Health Council 1996:29).

Another report suggests that approximately 66 per cent of the homeless population have had a diagnosis of mental illness at some point in their life. In addition, the prevalence of alcohol and substance abuse was about two-thirds. These figures were based on a survey of 300 single people using the Toronto hostels system (Emmanuel and Suttor 1998:32).

Deinstitutionalization has also been cited as a significant factor related to the increase in the numbers of homeless. Deinstitutionalization in which inpatient psychiatric patients were 'released' to community placements (with inadequate supports in place) occurred in the

1960s and 1970s, well before the rising tide of homelessness though. In Ontario, patients living in provincial asylums increased until 1960 to almost 20,000. By 1976 they numbered 5,000 (Rochefort 1997:226). Many of today's chronically mentally ill population would not have lived in former state-run mental health facilities. Instead, they have 'grown up in a milieu of psychiatric patient's rights movements, regulatory protection against involuntary commitment, and new medications' (Glasser and Bridgman 1999:52; see also Kiesler 1991).

Emphasis on mental illness (medical solutions for individual pathologies) takes attention away from homelessness (a social welfare problem inextricably linked to housing and economic opportunities) (see Aviram 1990). All the macro-level structural factors – for example, lack of affordable housing, shift in employment patterns associated with global restructuring, lack of educational opportunities, poverty, and shifting welfare provisions – combine with personal vulnerabilities (mental illness, substance abuse, histories of abuse or domestic violence) to render people homeless.

The most insightful writing on homelessness links individual experiences of homelessness with larger social processes and conditions. Involvement of drugs, mental illness, alcohol, prostitution, and crime in homeless people's lives should be viewed within broader contexts of poverty, lack of employment, lack of affordable housing, and neglect of social safety nets for all citizens.

Chronically Homeless Women

Many chronically homeless women live with mental illness, alcoholism, and drug use. Reports highlight their vulnerability to infectious diseases (such as tuberculosis and sexually transmitted diseases), poor nutrition, poor hygiene, foot problems, and leg ulcers. Homeless women have also been vulnerable to sexual abuse as children and to domestic abuse at the hands of their partners (D'Ercole and Struening 1990; Goldsack 1999; Novac, Brown, and Gallant 1999:8; Ritchey, La Gory, and Mullis 1991). Mental health problems and substance abuse have been found by some researchers to be associated with histories of childhood abuse (Bassuk et al. 1997; Herman et al. 1997; Koegel, Melamid, and Berman 1995; Smith and North 1994). Histories of abuse among homeless women prompt researchers, such as Annabel Tomas and Helga Dittmar (1995), to conclude that perhaps homelessness is not quite the problem that society at large understands it to be. Instead, unsafe housing is the problem, and homelessness becomes an adaptive survival strategy. Sylvia Novac argues that 'while men's homelessness is attributed primarily to unemployment, for women it is more likely to be family breakdown, and abuse by a husband or father' (1995:59). These kind of research findings are important, as they suggest the importance of women-only emergency facilities and sex-segregated housing forms (Novac, Brown, and Bourbonnais 1996:105).[4]

In their report on long-term homeless women, Sylvia Novac, Joyce Brown, and Gloria Gallant (1999) collated (self-reported) admissions data from three Toronto agencies – two women's shelters and a women's shelter outreach program. The report highlights the following key findings (p. 11):

- A disproportionate number of women were African Canadian.
- A high proportion of them had severe mental illness (perhaps half overall, although some did not receive any psychiatric treatment).
- Between 13 and 29 per cent of them had addictions.
- Between 9 and 42 per cent had been involved with the criminal justice system.
- Some 34 per cent were from racial minorities (including 23 per cent who are black); 37 per cent were immigrants.
- About 57 per cent were single and had never married.
- Another 39 per cent were divorced, separated, or widowed.
- A total of 48 per cent had completed high school or post-secondary education, while 16 per cent never even started high school.
- Most received income assistance (two women were employed part-time); nine had no income at all.
- Their ages ranged from sixteen to over sixty-five years, but 79 per cent were between twenty-five and fifty-four.
- Some 71 per cent of the women had been diagnosed with schizophrenia; the rest had other psychiatric disorders.
- About 58 per cent had been admitted as psychiatric patients at least once.

The report also includes ten profiles of long-term homeless women interviewed about their housing histories and experiences of homelessness. The researchers caution: 'Some long-term homeless women are extremely insular and antisocial and unwilling to be interviewed, especially those who have spent many years in a psychiatric hospital. These women's voices are ... missing from our interviews. They generally have severe mental health, not addiction, problems. Even when they are willing to talk to an interviewer, what they say may be difficult to understand or interpret ... [We] believe that our interview representation is somewhat skewed in that it reflects the experiences of women who are more communicative, socially connected, and willing to share their life stories' (p. 43).

The profiles attest to poverty, traumatic childhood, abuse and violence, unstable housing, a lack of sustained employment (and when employed, low-paid service jobs), mental health problems in parallel with addiction issues. Three brief profiles follow (from Novac, Brown, and Gallant 1999).

Hilda left home when she was 17 because her stepfather was abusing her physically, sexually, and emotionally. As a teenage mother, her first two children were 'taken away,' and she went through an emotional breakdown which was diagnosed as manic depression. She was hospitalized twice, and tried to commit suicide. In her twenties she had three more children who are now being raised by her mother in another city. She attributes her homelessness to her former partner who 'put [her] out on the street to work.' She has used Out of the Cold services [temporary winter shelters that offer mats on the floor] and stayed at various shelters off and on for ten years, with a more intensive three-year period that included sleeping rough. (p. 45)

Vicki left home when she was 16 years old because she and her mother were not getting along. For a short time, she lived on her home reserve and helped to raise her cousin's daughter and care for her cousin until her death from cancer. Returning to her mother's home in Toronto and finding their relationship unimproved, Vicki left for the street 'with everything she could shove in a gym bag.' Over the past several years she has generally stayed with friends. A couple of times, she and her boyfriend had a place of their own. She augmented their welfare cheque with panhandling, but they ended up in arrears anyway because he spent all their money on alcohol. She has been sleeping behind buildings under construction or in parking lots. When it got colder, she and her boyfriend, his brother, and another woman began staying at Out of the Cold sites. The four of them stay together, whether sleeping rough or staying in a shelter, and look out for each other. (p. 47)

Until six years ago, Marie was employed and had her own apartment.

When she was fired from her job, she began a wrongful dismissal complaint and applied for unemployment insurance. Once her savings were exhausted, the stress of the lawsuit and financial worries made it impossible for her to look for another job. She was drinking heavily and lost her apartment. She continued to pursue her lawsuit while living in a women's shelter for two months, but then gave up and left the shelter for the street. Since then she has stayed at only one other women's shelter, generally sleeping rough, and using drop-ins to sleep during the day. She used to spend all night in donut shops before finding a drop-in centre she liked. She avoids shelters because of her heavy drinking. Even when a shelter will accept her drinking, she finds it hard to make the curfew limits. On rare occasions she stays with a friend. (p. 51)

Some researchers capitalize on the strengths of homeless women and celebrate building upon their problem-solving skills (Montgomery 1994; Thrasher and Mowbray 1995). This is the approach that the Women Street Survivors Resource Group collectively drew upon: 'The strengths, skills and survival abilities of the women will be recognised and respected.' Reflecting on their commitment to the work at Savard's, three staff members testified in their interviews:

It should never be forgotten, and that's how I survive every day with as little judgment as humanly possible. I never forget that it could be me tomorrow that is living on the street, that is homeless, that has mental health issues. I could wake up tomorrow and be very, very ill. And I know from having a sister who's labelled 'schizophrenic,' that it's all very well and good to say, 'Oh, my God ... how can she live with this?' I'm a daughter of an alcoholic who killed herself through alcohol, so I have to remember, that could be me. I must never forget every day I walk through the door, that it could be me tomorrow, and as long as I remember that, then I think I can do justice to this work. If I forget that, then it's time ... [trailing off]

The second staff member attested:

My respect for the women we serve has increased [laughter]. Sometimes we do get really angry with S. – she can be a terrific pain. There are [laughter] days when I think, I gotta get out of here, but on the other hand, her survival, like her ability to survive is just phenomenal! She's smart. There's times that you can only admire her, and can only say, 'I don't think I could do it' [laughter]. I'd be *under now*. I'd be *gone*. I'd be *dead*. I couldn't do the things to survive.

Another staff member spoke passionately about how homeless women's behaviours had to be understood within a much larger framework of systemic oppression.

> The decision to have a sort of non-interventionist approach at Savard's arises out a distinct analysis of women's anger. That women will react, in angry ways or abusive ways or violent ways, or not socially acceptable ways, for very real reasons related to their oppression and that it is different than men's acting out.
>
> I think men also act out because of oppression, class oppression and all the rest of it, but women's anger is different, and requires a different approach. As women, we've all had our boundaries. We live with our boundaries being crossed, and it takes a lot of hard work to learn your own rights. For me, I don't like the word 'primitive,' but for me, when the women act out, it's a primitive reaction to their history of oppression, and what they perceive, what they perceive to be current oppression. We're second class citizens.

This staff member's position affirms the work of activists and researchers, such as Marion Pirie (1998), who advocate the recognition of feminist analyses of the causes of women's mental health problems and feminist approaches to intervention. Such analyses acknowledge that women's behaviours labelled pathological must be understood within larger contexts of systemic oppression and histories of abuse.

Shelters for Homeless Women

Many fine pieces of extended ethnographic study have been undertaken to tell the stories of individual homeless women, to share their daily strategies for surviving, and to explore their relationships with their families and with other homeless women (for example, Butler 1994; Harris 1991; Ross 1982). Homeless women's experiences in Canadian hostels have also been well documented through several ethnographic studies (Harman 1989; Farge 1989, 1988; Ross 1982). Issues related to social control, surveillance, and dependency echo in many of the studies: 'The action of workers' power over the residents – the threats, the surveillance, the repetition of rules, guiding and counselling – all must be understood within the context of the institutional imperative to run smoothly' (Farge 1988:88).

Elliot Liebow's book, *Tell Them Who I Am: The Lives of Homeless Women* (1993), is one of the few contemporary ethnographic studies of homelessness in which collaboration with the community under study was taken seriously, and literally. Liebow worked for ten years with the homeless women and staff of two shelters in Washington, D.C. – 'The Bridge' and 'The Refuge.' He included their commentaries and insights on his manuscript in footnotes throughout the book. Liebow highlights how homeless women who utilize shelters and hostels are frequently subject to questions, rules, and regulations that they find intolerable and degrading: having to answer questions was part of the price for being powerless. These issues have been well documented in other studies (Baxter and Hopper 1981; Williams 1996).

Staff, even the most dedicated and well-meaning, are bound inextricably within hierarchical systems and exercise degrees of control over the women that can be intimidating. Yet knowledge of the kinds of pressures and issues that staff face on a daily basis, and the kinds of supports that they themselves need in order to do their work, must be understood together with residents' perceptions of that work.

Jean Calterone Williams (1996) has also documented the institutional control and surveillance that are generally part of shelter life and staff world views. Entry requirements and shelter regulations can, in fact, 'cream' the shelter population through self-selection and agency-selection, so that the 'best' of the homeless population will be 'served.' In a similar fashion, a lot of the research on homelessness has concentrated on those who successfully access services. Williams juxtaposes forms of institutional control next to the small acts of resistance by homeless shelter residents and residents' evaluations of shelter and staff practices. This vestige, for so it appears to be, of control has been taken by marginalized women who possess remarkable urban survival skills.

Shelters for homeless women in Canada, first established in the 1970s and 1980s, were in part inspired by the philosophies and activism driving the women's movement and early feminist consciousness. Many women's shelters were opened in response to the growing awareness of the needs of abused women and their children. 'This meant establishing as homelike an atmosphere as possible, attempting to lessen the division between professional and client, and emphasizing an empowerment rather than charity model' (Novac, Brown, and

Bourbonnais 1996:15). The design of women's shelters thus departed dramatically from the large-scale dormitories that had historically been provided for homeless men.[5]

One of Savard's staff who had worked for many years with homeless women recounted some of this history:

> There's been a whole move now to regularize or formalize or institutionalize – 'shelterize' is the other word. The feminist shelters during the seventies were ground-breaking and wanting to break down the barriers. There was this whole kind of move to get away from all those professional boundaries of client and professional and have it more women exchanging experiences and empowering, through getting rid of those barriers. We were trying to involve the residents when there were staff meetings, to have them answering the phones, and involve women more with the operations of the shelter.
>
> I can actually recall a woman being quite suicidal on the phone and another resident taking the call, and dealing with it, and doing a better job than I could've done almost. Or the staff could've done, 'cause she knew the woman and knew how to handle it. ...
>
> Maybe it's just the pendulum swinging back and forth. I think it's partly the schools that are putting in the professional ethic. I think there have been situations of real abuse in the shelters between staff and residents, and a few of those incidents really changed everything for everybody else.
>
> Now, there are many more things in place that set the professional boundaries much more clearly. I guess it's also contributed to this huge bureaucracy of shelters in Toronto. Before there were just four or five. Now there are thirty, and they all have to have some kind of baseline rules for funding. And the hostel guidelines and procedures are really very extensive.
>
> So, on the one hand, there is a need for that, but on the other hand, it's just this institutionalization of the whole hostel system, and a move to that instead of permanent housing.

Other Initiatives for Ending Chronic Homelessness

Surveyed are what seem to be some promising Canadian examples for helping long-term homeless women – initiatives featured in the published literature on chronic homelessness. Included are drop-ins or daytime respites, case management strategies, shelters, transitional housing (generally consisting of housing with supports, for a limited period of time, say, several months to two years), and supportive housing (housing with supports for an open-ended period of time), as well as employment training.[6]

Daytime respites

Chez Doris in Montreal is a daytime respite for homeless women who may have psychiatric and/or substance abuse problems. It is multilingual (French, English, and Inuktitut). Sixty women come for food, clothing, bathing, laundry facilities, and the company of others each day. Staff are available and helpful, but respect the women's right to live as they want. The drop-in provides a 'low-demand, no-questions-asked' service. The women who use Chez Doris provide much of the labour for running the respite: 'Chez Doris, a day centre for women, was founded in 1977 by a group of community workers and other interested individuals who took to heart the poignant request of an alcoholic prostitute named Doris. Doris was often heard to say that she wished there was a place for women to get together for a cup of coffee and a bit of conversation safe from prying do-gooders and demanding male pimps and alcoholics. Doris was brutally murdered in 1974, so was never able to benefit from the many services offered at Chez Doris ... Chez Doris is an island of safety in an otherwise violent world' (Chez Doris, informational packet for volunteers, cited in Glasser and Bridgman 1999:49).

Another daytime respite or drop-in in Toronto, Sistering, provides individual and group support for homeless or transient women. Many of the women who use Sistering (more than 50 per cent) are chronic or ex-psychiatric patients. Breton (1984, 1989) highlights the fact that Sistering is part of a community centre that offers recreational and educational activities for the non-homeless public. Unlike many other facilities for the homeless, this one is not ghettoized or set apart. The process of 'normalization' requires that the women frequenting Sistering follow some basic rules of acceptable behaviour: 'After a short trial-and-error period, it was established that there would be no physical fights and no prolonged screaming and carrying-on: definite time-limits now exist for "blowing-up," and consequences of refusing to conform to behavioral expectations are enforced, albeit with com-

passion – the women have to leave the room and the Center temporarily' (Breton 1989:52).

The danger is that Sistering may lose the 'most alienated and needy
of the women it wants to serve' with these behavioural expectations
and sanctions (Breton 1989:53). Breton also suggests that there needs to
be a balance between offering help to women as individuals and
encouragement on the part of staff for women to form small mutual
aid groups and recognize their plight collectively (for example, the
inadequacy of support services for psychiatric survivors, homelessness, and domestic violence).

In 1990 Sistering expanded its operations and developed a second
site. The outreach service operates in the community centre setting.
The drop-in has its own site and serves approximately 100 women a
day. Sistering celebrated its twentieth anniversary in 2001 and now
offers a range of services and activities: advocacy and housing support,
an ID clinic (for helping women obtain identification documents),
health services (for example, foot care, and public health nurse visits),
and workshops offered in different languages (for example, Spanish
and Portuguese) for life skills and abuse issues. A community garden
has started, together with pottery, woodworking, and sewing workshops. Women's meetings are also held for those who are interested.

Case Management Strategies

One community-oriented case management strategy for homeless
women in Montreal has been studied by Céline Mercier and Guylaine
Racine (1995). They analyse the daily contact logs of two case managers serving twenty-five homeless and formerly homeless women
associated with Maison l'Invitée, a Montreal detoxification and rehabilitation centre for homeless women with substance addictions. There
are 11,104 contacts with the twenty-five women analysed in the study.
The case management services operate from an office in an apartment
in downtown Montreal. These services generally focus on building and
maintaining relationships, help with finding housing, and money
management. The apartment does not function merely as a professional contact setting, but more as a 'community living room' (Segal
and Baumohl 1985) for the women in the program: 'clients meet there
to share a meal, organize and take part in recreational activities, or simply take a break from their turbulent lives' (Mercier and Racine
1995:27).

Interestingly, only 20 per cent of the meetings with the women take place *outside* the office context, despite the so-called community orientation of this project. Glasser and Bridgman suggest a potential lesson from the study: 'even with a "community" orientation, some programs revert to the more traditional office setting unless conscious steps are taken to keep this from happening' (1999:97).

Mercier and Racine set out to gather empirical data on how case management programs actually function. They admit that a large number of women left the program not long after joining it, and only those women who stayed in the programme at least six months are part of their study. They caution that: 'the difficulty of the recruiting process reinforces the acknowledged difficulty of keeping the homeless in support programs. The impact of such difficulties on the programs themselves must not be under-estimated' (1995:28).

Shelters

Sandy Merriman House offers a fifteen-bed overnight shelter and a drop-in program in a restored heritage home in downtown Victoria, British Columbia. The shelter serves approximately 470 women a year, with the average length of stay being eight days, while the drop-in serves over 1,000 women yearly. The facility is one of ten Canadian best practices identified by the Canada Mortgage and Housing Corporation (1999b:5–20). Twelve women on social assistance were trained in basic carpentry skills and helped with the construction phase of the project.

Sandy Merriman House serves homeless women, many of whom are dealing with severe and persistent mental illness. Many work in the sex trade. The house operates with a peer-support model recognizing that 'the women it serves have typically had negative experiences with institutions and mainstream services' (Canada Mortgage and Housing Corporation 1999b:5). Staff offer support and advice only when it is requested. A broad range of services are offered through the shelter and drop-in: one-on-one support, referrals to community resources and services, life skills workshops, weekly on-site street nurse services, daily meal, addictions support groups, and computer access.

The Canada Mortgage and Housing Corporation report includes the following 'client story' from Sandy Merriman House (pp. 12–13):

Martha had an abusive childhood, was abandoned by her mother and was entrenched in the street lifestyle by the age of 14. She came to the SMH with a long history of violent relationships, intravenous cocaine and heroin use, work in the sex trade and legal problems.

Martha frequently used the Shelter and the Drop-In services, and came to trust the staff. Before reaching out for help she hit bottom: one day at the Drop-In, under the influence of drugs and feeling suicidal, she ran out of the building into oncoming traffic. Subsequently, she approached staff asking for support and was assisted in the following areas:

access to appropriate legal and health services

harm reduction and lifestyle change; and

access to a detox centre and recovery house.

Martha ... stopped working the streets and learned to care about and for herself. She secured her own home. She participated in a community training program ... and went on to obtain a certificate in life skills training. As of January 1999, she was employed by a community organization, in a healthy relationship and attending Narcotics Anonymous.

Transitional Housing

Transitional housing generally consists of housing with supports. The time period is limited, and varies from several months to two years. The Native Women's Transition Centre (opened in 1981) in Winnipeg, Manitoba, has been recognized by the Canada Mortgage and Housing Corporation (1999b:45–55) as a best practice. The project provides long-term residential services for Aboriginal women who have experienced family violence, abuse, addiction, involvement with Child and Family Services, and inadequate housing.

This long-term residential facility (four rooms and three suites accommodating twenty-one residents) is staffed twenty-four hours a day and is a safe home for Native women and their children. Staff are all Aboriginal women. There are ex-residents among the full and part-time staff, and on the board of directors. The program respects traditional Native practices. The healing circle is an integral part of its program, and a healing room has been built to resemble a teepee. Generally the maximum length of stay is one year.

After one year, residents may choose to move on to second-stage housing at Memengwaa Place ('Home of the Butterfly'). Memengwaa Place opened in 1994, provides a more independent living arrangement, and has seven full suites, an on-site support worker, and security features. Here is one story:

My name is Bernice ... [My] children were picked up by Child and Family Services (CFS) in 1993. I was trying to fight for my children on my own. Two years later, I realized I was losing the battle and that CFS had plans to take my children as permanent wards. I felt like an empty shell walking around. I felt very troubled and very lost. Then I ran into a worker from the Native Women's Transition Centre and I began telling her about my situation and how helpless I felt. I told her I was ready to give up the fight for my children and therefore the fight for my life ...

I found that the NWTC had many programs. I became involved with all their programs and also received one-to-one counselling. In addition, I also began therapy with a psychologist. With this much-needed support, I began to change into a strong person.

As a result, I will be getting my children back ... and now I do not feel so empty. I have learned to live a sober lifestyle and now I realize I no longer need alcohol and drugs ...

Another exciting thing happening in my life is the opportunity to get involved with community issues. Before this, I never knew much or even cared about what community meant. My thoughts were to make ends meet from day to day. I didn't bother anyone and I didn't want anyone to bother me. If I didn't like my neighbours, I moved. Now I see I can be part of a community by getting involved.

Supportive Housing

Supportive housing offers accommodation for an open-ended period of time, such as Memengwaa Place above. Studies led by Sylvia Novac suggest that as many as a quarter of homeless women, precariously housed women, or women living in supportive housing projects would prefer to live in women-only buildings, including private-sector rooming houses. Yet there are very few women-only supportive housing buildings or projects, for example, in Toronto. Just 6 per cent of supportive housing units in Toronto are designed specifically for women (Novac, Brown, and Gallant 1999:59). Significantly, those living in these projects report higher levels of satisfaction and fewer problems than women living in non-segregated projects (Novac et al. 1996).

A report issued by Status of Women Canada (Johnson and Ruddock 2000), *Building Capacity: Enhancing Women's Economic Participation through Housing*, surveys Canadian housing-related initiatives for alleviating women's poverty. The authors, Laura Johnson and Allison Ruddock, confirm the obvious – that without secure, stable, and affordable housing, it is more difficult for women to care for their children, seek employment training, pursue educational goals, or enter the labour force. They highlight an uncommon model of supportive government-assisted housing projects – those that offer housing-based employment training. It would be important to ensure that security of tenure in such housing is not tied to mandatory participation, however (see Wekerle 1993:108).

Among ten promising case studies in the Status of Women Canada report, Five by Five, in Prince Albert, Saskatchewan, enables five single mothers on social assistance to buy and renovate homes through a cooperative structure. The women qualify for a provincial training program to learn about co-operative management, home-ownership responsibilities, and basic construction skills (Johnson and Ruddock 2000:45–46).

At the time of writing this book, there was a study under way (with a team lead by Dara Culhane and Rebecca Bateman) of a new social housing project for women in Vancouver's downtown eastside neighbourhood. Forty-eight units of permanent, emergency, and transitional housing were being developed by the Bridge Housing Society for Women. The study was to document and analyse the effects that living in the Bridge community would have on the health of residents, many of whom would be Aboriginal and homeless.

Gerda Wekerle identified over fifty women-developed and women-controlled Canadian housing projects (approximately 1,500 units) and conducted in-depth case studies of ten of those women's housing projects: 'Women's housing projects have given women the opportunity to become active agents within a housing system that excludes them as developers, builders, managers or owners of housing ... Using state-funded housing programs, women's groups have managed to house some of the most marginalized women: elderly women, single parents, teenage mothers, abused women and their children. The numbers of units built are a drop in the bucket compared to the need, but the existence of actual projects developed by and run by women for women in communities across Canada, are important signposts of women's initiative and perseverance' (Wekerle 1993:111; see also Wekerle and Novac 1989).

Conclusion

All the above approaches have been targeted to the needs of homeless women and low-income women at risk of losing their housing. They recognize that many homeless women who have experienced violence, abuse, and instability in their housing have turned to the shelter system for refuge, while others have turned to the streets.

Within the literature on chronically homeless women suffering from mental illness, words such as 'non-compliant' feature. They are also labelled as 'service resisters' and 'the hard to reach' (Cohen 1992). These women are identified as having 'problems,' as being social 'problems,' and their homelessness is a 'problem.' The standard question asked by many in society is, 'Why would you be giving help to people who aren't asking for help?' This question assumes that people are 'choosing' to live outside and that they have the privilege of making a 'choice.' In fact, many people are caught in cycles of homelessness, and their choices are limited. Brenda Doyle Farge (1989:144) is harsh about homeless women having 'freedom of choice.' She writes: 'A woman who is frightened is not free. Much of the language of choice is simply a justification for not dealing with marginalized women at the level of their needs ... [Such] terminology has the effect of masking the years of damage done to them, damage often at the hands of the men in their lives: fathers, brothers, husbands, landlords, and employers. ... They are not well educated; they are not middle class; they do not have the tools needed to function well in a competitive world. Women like this are knocked over and over again. And in the end it is said of them, "Well, they've made their choices."'

Turn questions about 'resistance' and 'non-compliance' round. Ask, what is it that the women are resisting? Why are the shelters or services not working for them? In exercising what Breton (1994) describes as 'negative power' – the ability to withhold participation, consent, and involvement in programs designed by 'expert others' for them – these women step outside structures and limits set by others.

With the failure of services to engage homeless people, 'non-traditional,' low-demand, gradual approaches have been developed (Barrow et al. 1992; Susser, Goldfinger, and White 1990; Lovell and Cohn 1998). Anne Lovell and Sandra Cohn highlight how notions of empowerment, and terms such as *client-driven* or *client-oriented* have come into vogue since the 1980s in mental health services (1998:8–9). They join others in being critical, though, of the rhetoric around these concepts, when input from the homeless does not necessarily translate into action or meaningful choices.

Resistance refers not only to resistance on the part of homeless women, however. Resistance can also refer to opposition on the part of service providers. Frank Lipton suggests that the 'concept of safe havens [involves] an effort to simultaneously grapple with client resistance and program resistance. The resistance of homeless individuals to participate in services and the resistance of many existing programs to serving clients who do not fit neatly into the models which have been created' (1993:20).

Dennis Culhane's (1997) research in the United States highlights the fact that while the chronic homeless are only about 10 per cent of shelter users, they consume 50 per cent of the [emergency] shelter system days. They therefore represent about half of the sheltered population on any given day. Culhane concludes that the chronically homeless should be the target of permanent housing programs (1997).

Savard's represents one such innovative housing program that attempts to offer chronically homeless mentally ill women an opportunity to 'come inside' and begin the (long) processes of healing. Savard's also addresses the 'lack of effective housing programs for women ... [and] the fact that women have had relatively little role or input in the design or management of Canadian housing programs ... [that] have been developed and managed mostly by men' (SPR Associates 1998:29). Savard's has been developed primarily by women for women.

CHAPTER FOUR

Safe Haven: The Vision

This is true virtue ...
to listen, to argue, to wade on through the muck
wrestling to some momentary small agreement
like a pinhead pearl prized from a dragon-oyster.

Marge Piercy, 'Report of the Fourteenth Subcommittee on Convening a Discussion Group'[1]

'Safe Haven: The Vision' explores initial planning discussions and decisions about the nature of the Women Street Survivors Project. Those working on the project conceived of it as a radical alternative to current paradigms of shelter provision for chronically homeless women in Toronto. They were knowledgeable about the limitations of other shelters, programs, and funding arrangements, and drew collectively on years of experience in 'the sector.'

This chapter explores the vision – the questions, debates, and uncertainties. 'Whom are you not able to serve, and why not?' How could women with a history of violent behaviour be helped, when they did not seem to 'fit in' elsewhere in the 'system'? Two particular questions are explored. Each is linked to the other.

The first question circles around the concepts of zero eviction and non-intervention that featured prominently in many discussions. How did these ideas intersect with very real concerns about dealing creatively with homeless women's potentially violent behaviour?

The second question involves definitions of transitional housing, conventional profiles of shelter provision, ideas about permanency, and even a sense of 'home' for the women. What does *safe haven* mean?

Violence, Non-intervention, and Eviction

Following is an abridged excerpt from a transcript of a Women Street Survivors Resource Group meeting late in 1996. Top on the agenda that day were issues of violence, and debate about current institutionalized routines of 'barring' or eviction practised by so many other shelters. Should women be barred from (not allowed to return to) the house for incidents of violence?

> 16 October 1996, 1:30 – 2:45 p.m.
> Women Street Survivors Resource Group
> 10 in attendance, then 2 others arrived later

> [Notes: Sometimes the scraping of chairs obliterated words. Someone had a bad cold and was coughing a lot. The sound of trucks outside interfered with taping. The security buzzer also sounded several times, as other people arrived for the meeting.]

A M I E : I think we need to list the principles separately here. One that's not listed in the minutes of the last meeting – which could be the most controversial – zero eviction.

J O A N : It's an issue – an issue to discuss.

A M I E : Well, no. It's a principle.

J O A N : I know. We have to discuss it first as an issue *before* we put it down as a principle.

M A R I A : Security and tenure [voice trailing off, coughing].

A M I E : That's the hole that you start to make bigger and bigger over time. The issue is – do you shut the door right now, and you adopt an absolute position? From that position, you are coerced forever to address the issue. There's no escape hatch. You can't create an escape hatch for yourself.

L E E : Zero eviction is tough on the staff. It's pretty tough on the staff [laughter]. Here, you take it! [laughter]

A M I E : This project is tough on everybody. But as a principle, zero eviction holds everybody accountable. These are people we're saying can't live anywhere else.

L E E : We need to talk a little bit more about it, before we make that statement.

A M I E : I'm not advocating for it one way or another. What must permeate all of this operation is the sense of accountability towards the women – the women who have had the most difficulty. The more little loopholes you create, though, the wider they get over time. It's that way by nature.

MARGARET: Why is it that people like Margaret T. have to leave? What would have made a difference?

JOAN: There's a reason why these women aren't using services. They are very frightening and threatening to other people. And some of that threatening behaviour may be very defensive. As they get to feel more comfortable and build up trust, they may be able to learn other ways of relating. Being threatening can be a defence; it can make you feel safe. The reason why Margaret T. gets kicked out – all the behaviour that people wouldn't put up with – is that she won't stop stealing everybody else's belongings. That's what does it in the end. People are very tolerant of the door slamming and all the noise [violent scraping sounds as Joan knocks one of the chairs about] [laughter]. But when people start catching her with their cheques *and* their ID *and* their keys *and* everything ...

JOAN: For her, it isn't stealing. It is – you know, *hers* ...

LEE: I would like a basis to start working from, rather than just being thrown into a new project. I need some assumptions given to me that I can either choose or throw out. Even if you have tons of experience in other projects, this is a whole unique, different kind of a place – so your experiences may or may not be relevant. They can be applied, but they might not work. Women that will be using this space have another whole level of responses in the way that they use space. I don't want to be saying, 'Go out there, and make up the rules as you go along.' There's that tension – between what as a staff you need going into a position like this and a woman who hasn't used any services before.

CARRY: And what the purpose of the project is as well.

LEE: You have to merge all of those three maybe conflicting needs together.

MARIA: It's hard to balance. Having no expectations of the women who come in, with personal security and safety of the staff, with our 'Let's learn, let's be flexible, let's whatever' with [voice trailing off].

CARRY: And it involves the safety of the other women, as well.

MARIA: How flexible can you be [laughter]?

CARRY: If we have a woman who is threatening, or targeting a particular person, and compromising safety, do we bar her, or do we find some way of working with her, or do we ask her to leave temporarily?

PAM: Some women want rules. They want to know what they are, they want to know what they are, right from the start. It can be a very mysterious process about how long someone can stay ... 2 weeks, 3 weeks, 1 year, whatever it is. When is it okay for someone to take over a space? Who decides? Things are decided for them. They have to ask for everything they need. They have to ask for soap, shampoo. They're infantilized.

MARGARET: We have the obligation not to let our staff be killed or hurt. And we also have the same obligation to the women residents. This can't be a place where people come and get hurt.

MARIA: But the project assumes that a lot of these women are being barred from other places for some of their behaviour. We have a higher level of tolerance for some of that, by virtue of what the project is.

TINA: Our definition of our own personal safety is very different for each of us.

MARGARET: If there is going to be a higher level of tolerance, there will be greater risks.

MARIA: I guess my operating assumption has been that we wouldn't be barring them. That other places would bar women, but we wouldn't.

PAM: That's right.

MARIA: So, do we bar women?

TINA: If somebody hits a staff person at another place, they're barred. If they hit a staff person in this project, will they be barred? How would we respond?

JOAN: I.think no barring is an important concept. That doesn't mean that women don't leave. They may have to go to the hospital. You may have to call the police. That's happened – for someone who's totally out of control. There may be reasons that women have to leave the space. But that's different than barring. Maybe they get some kind of medication that changes their behaviour, and they come back. I would rather seeing a 'no-barring policy' – which doesn't preclude other ways of removing women when they need to be removed.

This exchange represents but one of many such discussions. Acknowledged throughout the meetings were a number of difficulties. Experience that staff bring to the workplace may or may not work with the projected population. Women living in the project may not respond in expected ways. In a context of experimentation and an expressed mission to learn from homeless women themselves, how could staff not fall into the trap of 'making up the rules as we go along'?

One disgruntled front-line worker commented to me informally several days after the meeting: 'I couldn't say anything negative at that meeting, could I? Give something – even the most basic rule – but give something! You can scream at me, you can even push me, but you can't hit me, and you can't hit other residents. Take that and build on it. Start with what you've got and build on it. We're not operating in a vacuum, where we don't know nothing. Staff are going to need an incredible amount of support in maintaining that *non-line*.'

She went on to tell a story about Ruby, who lived in another shelter she had worked at. The story challenged what she perceived as the apparent free-for-all 'anything goes' philosophy being proposed for the Women Street Survivors Project. At issue in the anecdote are ideas about competence, responsibility, and structure. Ruby had questioned this staff worker about why the rules had been ignored when Sarah, another shelter resident, transgressed one of the facility's rules. She said to me, 'You're taking away my responsibility. You're taking away Sarah's responsibility. She's just as *crazy* as *I* am!'

That particular meeting of the Women Street Survivors Resource Group was held but a scant two and a half months before the project opened in January 1997. The impetus for such debates, however, had its start years before.

The Start

In 1985, the Mayor's Task Force on Homelessness in Toronto recognized that many people with serious mental health issues were using temporary emergency hostels as permanent shelter. The catalyst for action being taken on this knowledge was the freezing death later that year of Drina Joubert, and the subsequent coroner's inquest into her death. In part because of the inquest's recommendations, several services to address gaps in support for homeless people suffering from serious mental illness were put in place. Some of these were geared to women specifically and included Joubert House, Margaret Frazer House, and Cornerstone. Two safe drop-in spaces for women were also set up. The Hostel Outreach Program (HOP) was initiated in order to provide ongoing support to individuals with mental health issues, who were living in hostels but were unable to access services on their own.

Even with these kinds of supports in place, many front-line shelter workers were concerned about a growing number of long-term homeless women who seemed unable, or unwilling, to access or participate in support and treatment programs. Nor were these women able to live in existing emergency hostel or housing options. Some were seen as 'too difficult' and were asked to leave hostels for what was considered aggressive or bizarre behaviour. Many were not able to go through (intrusive) intake processes for supportive housing, nor could they comply with the myriad rules and expectations required by many housing providers (for example, observing set curfews, attending regimented day programs, signing contracts about their goals, or complying with administration of medications). Some of the women's propensity for hoarding, screaming, setting fires, and acts of violence against themselves and others also left them unable to access existing services. They often could not sleep with doors closed, and many wanted to sleep under tables or close to groups. Shelters and hostels had a low staffing ratio and were unable to deal with these women who were barred because of the amount of attention they needed. Other women at the shelters and hostels were also frightened by what they perceived as dangerous women.

One of the few alternatives for these women would be a mental health facility. Too often this could become a form of housing for these women, where they were institutionalized, medicated, and removed from society.

Discussion among women's services about the gap began in earnest in 1993, when the Women Street Survivors Resource Group was created. The group brought together front-line workers from approximately fifteen Toronto agencies including Nellie's, Street Haven, Regent Park Community Health Centre, 416 Drop-In, Sistering, Women's Residence, StreetCity, The Meeting Place, The Gerstein Centre, Rendu House, and HOP. The City of Toronto, through its Healthy City Office and the Departments of Housing and Public Health, Queen Street Mental Health Centre, Levitt Goodman Architects, and Metro Hostel Services also contributed human and financial resources.

When members of the Women Street Survivors Resource Group began to meet, they did not yet have a site. At the same time their meetings began, however, the Homes First Society was developing StreetCity Too (now known as Strachan House). The idea that a project for women street survivors might be incorporated into that project began to take shape. This strategy was a 'convenient' one as a member of the Women Street Survivors Resource Group put it. It meant that there would be tolerant neighbours, accepting of the kind of population that the project would be serving.

A major obstacle, obviously, was how to fund such a project. In September 1996, the Ministry of Health granted Homes First permission to use $100,000 of unused funds to get the Women Street Survivors

Project off the ground. HOP also agreed to do street outreach for the project and to coordinate the referrals.

One of the staff in the Community Housing Initiatives Section of the City of Toronto Housing Department had read an academic paper about Women of Hope in the autumn of 1994. The article by Dennis Culhane (1992), was entitled 'Ending Homelessness among Women with Severe Mental Illness: A Model Program from Philadelphia.' A low-demand respite was developed by a group of nuns, the Sisters of Mercy, and Catholic Social Services. The women they were trying to reach were identified as being mentally ill and labelled as 'non-compliant.' They were not using existing social and health services, nor were they using prescription drugs to modify and control behaviour. Women of Hope had reportedly had great success in helping chronically homeless mentally ill women make the transition from street life. At first, the women received blankets while they were living on the street, or they came in briefly for meals or a respite from the street. Gradually, many made more permanent moves. From 1985 until 1991, approximately 120 women were brought in off the street.

Copies of Dennis Culhane's paper were distributed to co-workers in the Community Housing Initiatives Section. A great deal of interest was generated in thinking about ways to house long-term homeless street women in Toronto. One of the HOP staff, Sheryl Lindsay, had attended a conference in Philadelphia in the spring of 1993 and visited Women of Hope while there. She was invited to attend the City's Alternative Housing Subcommittee to report on her impressions and findings about the Women of Hope program.

According to Lindsay's report ('Notes from Visit to "Women of Hope," Philadelphia, April 1993'), Women of Hope was based in an old schoolhouse inside a poor working-class district that was just beginning to be 'yuppified.' The building was leased from the Holy Ghost Fathers and operated by the Sisters of Mercy with funding from the Philadelphia Department of Health, and licensed as a personal care boarding house. The nuns did not do outreach themselves; outreach workers brought the women in. The facility had a connection to a mental health centre, and staff would come in and introduce themselves to the women.

A key element of Women of Hope's approach was that there would be no expectations for treatment or medication imposed on the women. Staff would advise women of their options, but felt that the women would return to the streets if they were forced to take medications. Women were able to come and go as they pleased. They were told that a bed would be held open for them for two weeks after last contact. A number of women were unable to sleep in beds after many years on the street. Some slept on the floor and some in chairs. If any woman was deemed dangerous, Women of Hope would facilitate admission to a psychiatric facility. The older women generally moved on to nursing homes. Staff believed that this type of housing was practical, and there should be no expectations that all women would eventually move on.

There was significant neighbourhood resistance to Women of Hope, and because of this, Women of Hope was unable to get permanent housing status. Lindsay's report included a number of recommendations about how Women of Hope would have done things differently, if they were to start over again. A limit of fifteen women would be the ideal size (rather than twenty-four). They would have facilitated women going out into the community for activities. Many of the women tended to stay in and watch television or sleep. They would have tried to advise residents about their choices and options more. They also would have developed criteria about who would stay and who would move on.

Impressed by what they had heard, a Toronto group of front-line workers, staff from Homes First, and municipal housing officials arranged to visit Philadelphia in January 1995 (ten years after the project originally opened) to see for themselves what was working well at Women of Hope. It seemed that the project had shifted substantially from its original mandate. Sisters of Mercy were no longer involved with the project and management of the project had changed. Many residents were now medicated, and participation in treatment and programming was mandatory.

Women of Hope became part of the U.S. national strategy adopted by the McKinney Act on Homelessness, defined as a 'Continuum of Care.' Dennis Culhane's paper is but one of several written in the early 1990s that focused on the safe haven model in the United States. In another paper, Frank Lipton (1993:3–4) attempted to define the parameters of *a safe haven* clearly.[2]

A haven does not merely refer to the literal place where refuge is provided but to certain characteristics which are necessary in order to make an individual feel safe and secure such as lack of excessive demands, consistency, easy accessibility, flexibility, continuity, individualized attention, ability to make choices, and cultural relevance.

A safe haven provides a sense of decency, caring and dignity. It's an environment which makes an individual feel comfortable and at home. It is free of violence, crime and victimization. A haven is the people one talks to for support, encouragement, and guidance; the activities one participates in; the services one can depend on; knowing that there's a place to sleep, food to eat, money to survive, clothes to wear, access to health care, medications to take.

Safe havens are, in a sense, a metaphor for community support systems ... Safe havens are proposed as a type of facility which would serve as a potential 'portal of entry' to the service system. Safe havens are viewed as 'transitional' housing programs which will provide individuals with the opportunity to develop essential skills, be linked to community based supports, and overcome the obstacles necessary to successfully obtain housing.

Of interest in this definition is the clear emphasis on the safe haven as a transitional 'portal of entry' to a range of services with the eventual aim of leading to conventional housing. The continuum of care is designed to stream outreach services attached to an emergency shelter system. The traditional housing continuum expects linear progression from outreach through to shelter, transitional housing, supportive housing, long-term housing, and eventually, private market housing.

Disappointed, the Toronto group returned from Philadelphia. They resolved that they did not wish to repeat what they called 'The Philadelphia Story.' The trip reinforced the value of the approach that activists in Toronto wished to take. Writing in one of the City of Toronto Housing Department's newsletters, the then chief official in the Housing Department, Bob Yamashita (1995), outlined the larger context for Women of Hope.

Yamashita critiqued the continuum of care as 'an attempt to rationalize [the U.S.] service network by producing "stable" tenants for the private rental market.' Further, the kind of outreach that the Toronto group witnessed was perceived as 'an aggressive campaign to clean up the streets' and emergency shelters became 'places to stabilize, medicate, detoxify, etc.'

In contrast, Toronto's model was defined by Yamashita as a community development continuum that centred around the homeless person as an individual and as a member of a community. Self-help initiatives and community development approaches recognize the strengths and potential that homeless people may bring to projects. The continuum within U.S. policy features a close-ended linked system that an individual must *move through* within a designated time-frame. The 'continuum' within the Toronto context was interpreted rather as a set of open-ended options to be used, when and if the person chooses to use them. In this context, intervention and assistance in Street Patrol outreach, for example, should be given only when requested.

For many of the Toronto organizers of Savard's, the Women of Hope visit became 'a clear reminder of the need to maintain the integrity of founding principles for the Street Survivors project' (Yamashita 1995). One member of the Women Street Survivors Resource Group declared: 'We don't have to go elsewhere to find models and experience. The models are here. The question is – how to free yourself from what you already know? We have that expertise right here in Toronto. We don't want to get caught in our own creeping assumptions. Zero eviction – it's a basic principle that we accept homeless women as they are, without expecting change – *without the expectations of change.'*

Housing, Hostel, or Home?

The shared goal of the Women Street Survivors Resource Group was to work through the safe haven model – a model premised on unlimited stay, a low-demand environment, and high support from staff. The model would allow time to engage individuals, assess their physical and mental health needs and their social service needs, and help them link up with appropriate community resources. A safe haven was understood to be a potentially permanent housing option, or individuals could choose to move into more independent housing, but at their own pace.

The members of the Women Street Survivors Resource Group had a general sense that the women were very isolated. It was assumed that the women would come and go. They would be living outside the system, for example, they would not receive government Family Benefits Allowance (FBA) or welfare benefits. They would not have using existing facilities. They might not have a lot of communication or interaction with each other, or with staff. One front-line worker suggested, 'You've got to find that person's metaphors. You don't have stay there in that place, but you have to be able to get inside.' Another expressed concern and asked a key question: 'How does this not become housing for those who could cope within the hostel system?'

The members of the Women Street Survivors Resource Group debated whether staff hired for the Women Street Survivors Project should be women only or women and men. Although some of the front-line workers spoke about a few women they had known who only spoke to male staff in shelters, the decision was that it would be simpler if only women were to be hired. Many homeless women have been abused by men as children, lovers, and wives.

Some of the front-line workers suggested that women might use the facility more as a drop-in 'clubhouse' or storage place for their belongings. There were, however, many discussions in planning meetings about how the house might, in fact, become a 'home' for some of the women living there, especially with the women's security and tenure being assured through a no-barring policy. That said, there was also considerable interest in the group about what 'home' may mean for the women. One of the members commented, 'Home is a refuge for most of us, but for many street women, home may be the most feared place.'

One member of the group tried to summarize discussion to that point: 'This is not a hostel. Does it matter if someone sleeps on a bed or sits on a chair, or sleeps on the floor?' Another responded, 'If this is going to evolve into a home – a safe space – we cannot give their space away!' A third said, 'They'll be part of a community whether they want to or not – what if they don't want to be?' A fourth followed with, 'Our roles are dictated by funding. It's all connected. We can't double-dip [i.e., charge a per diem] if Mary-Jane is staying at another hostel. And Mary-Jane has many names! [laughter].'[3]

The potential for the Women Street Survivors Project to evolve as a 'permanent' form of housing was clearly at odds with funding mandates for shelters dictating that they be 'transitional' only. The expectation on the part of potential funders was that the women would be encouraged to move on to other forms of housing. The Women Street Survivors Resource Group, therefore, presented the project as transitional for the purposes of attracting funding. Yet, this was done with the recognition that conventional time limits on length of stay, pressures to 'make progress,' and payment of housing charges had all been identified by the Women Street Survivors Resource Group as barriers for many chronically homeless women. 'You could have ten people who are not there? The women may come and go. A woman may stay, then flee in the middle of the night. A woman may stay one night, then be gone for three months.' Another member responded, 'Then the concept will change. This is a model we're trying to predict. Are we getting caught in a trap? To expect women to come in and stay ... we don't know the patterns because these women are not accessing the shelters.' The first member countered:

> We're going to need to work this out with Hostel Services – what they're willing, what's their flexibility? Is this a hostel or housing? And what are the implications? How long do we hold a room? How many women? What if there are more people than beds? What about vacancy versus demand for funding income? What kind of info do we pass along to women when we do outreach? Do they get a key? ... The money is coming from Hostel Services but it's not a hostel. It's not a hostel, but it is a hostel? [laughter] It's permanent, but they can come back when they've left? We want it to evolve. How do we present, 'This is your home. You can stay as long as you want'?

Another member chimed in: 'And at what point do women start to participate? What's the process of decision-making with residents? You know, many women with mental health problems are tremendously supportive and tolerant of each other.'

On many occasions during development meetings, someone would express uncertainty. 'We don't know the answers. We have ideas, but we don't know if they will work. We'll have to learn, learn from the women themselves. The need can be identified only when the need has been met – it *is* a backwards kind of process. But we have to reach some consensus. This period is over. We have to sign off on the process now.'

The questions revolved around many issues: definitions and distinctions between transitional housing and more permanent models; the degree of flexibility in existing funding mandates and associated definitions; outreach strategies, so that the project did not just become housing for those who could already cope within the hostel system; issues around twenty-four-hour staffing (for example, ensuring unified team work, a common vision, similar values, and consistency in applying founding guidelines); fitting in with external time lines for building construction; operating guidelines; and strategies for supporting both residents and staff.

There was the necessity of presenting a solid proposal about the

Women Street Survivors Project for outside organizations and funding agencies, for example, to justify flexibility around sign-in processes and per diem charges (for example, whereby residents would not be required to sign the pink shelter forms).[4] Setting the Women Street Survivors Project to paper provided an external foil to a more organic and internal 'it will come from the women themselves' approach, advocated by some members of the Women Street Survivors Resource Group. This flexibility, reflexivity, and openness to *change* and *evolution* nevertheless permeated planning for the Women Street Survivors Project, and it was enshrined in the project's First Principles.

Founding Ideals

The Women Street Survivors Resource Group drafted up a series of 'First Principles' for the Women Street Survivor Project. These were issued in late 1996, just as the project was about to open, and were included in the 'Women Street Survivors Project Orientation Manual.'

The principles challenged the conventions of shelter provision that society at large offers those who have experienced years of homelessness, anguish, mental illness, and substance addictions. Those conventions take the form of discrete hours of operation, curfews, and other elements of social control and coercion, through searching of personal possessions, the threat of permanent barring, mandatory treatment programs, mandatory regulations governing acceptable behaviours, the performance of chores, time limits on length of stay, requirements for bathing, and so on.

The project aimed to support a small group of women living on the street that were the most difficult to serve. The idea was to provide a model with 'some degree of stability, including a place to sleep, get food, access health care, and to find life skills support and companionship, be safe and out of the cold' (Women Street Survivor Project, Project Description, October 1996). In the words of one of the Women Street Survivors Resource Group, 'We don't want to intrude on the lives of the women. We're available, but we don't intervene.'

The model was one premised upon non-interventionist principles. Women would not be forced to seek psychiatric care, nor would they be coerced into treatment or training programs.

This orientation dovetailed with the philosophy of the Homes First Society. One of the administrators of the Homes First Society explained some of the striking differences between Homes First and other housing and shelter providers:

> With those other groups, you have to comply with certain things and those certain things can include: you can't drink here, you have to behave yourself, and if you want to stay for a longer period of time, then you have to have a plan, be committed to changing your life, overcoming your alcoholism, look for a job, getting your life together. We will help you and support you to do that, but there's a whole process of growth and change that you have to commit to, as a condition of being part of our environment ... If you don't follow the treatment regimen or you decide you don't want to go that way any more, you lose your housing as well, because your housing and your treatment are tied.
>
> But it's part of the philosophy of Homes First, our willingness to provide housing for people, it's unconditional. You don't have to commit to change. You don't have to commit to stop drinking. You don't have to commit to a plan-for-progress. The Homes First philosophy is that your need and your right to housing are separate from whatever else might be going on in your life.

Women Street Survivors Project
First Principles

> *There is a significant increase in the homeless population of Toronto which includes a small but growing number of street women who are chronically homeless. Many of these women, labelled/identified with serious mental health problems, are unable or unwilling to access or participate in existing treatment, support, hostel or housing programs. The structures, settings, environments and expectations of these programs do not meet the needs or wants of the women. It is a population of women that few, if any, housing programs can successfully and consistently house. The Project will be an opportunity to learn with women street survivors how to provide shelter and supports that will build on their capacities and strengths, meet their needs as they identify them, and improve the quality of the women's lives.*

> *This is a project that will evolve and change as the women involved teach, educate and inform us about their strengths, abilities, issues, needs, wants and perspectives.*

> *The space will be an 'envelope' that will respond to the ways in which the women want to live or be in it. The space will 'fit' the women rather than the women 'fitting' into the space.*

No rules (other than what is necessary for health and safety) or treatment/ program requirements will be placed on the women. There will be no expectations placed on the women to change. A flexible, non-judgmental, low-demand atmosphere and structure will be provided.

The strengths, skills, and survival abilities of the women will be recognized and respected. They will determine what, if any, supports, programs and services they want.

CHAPTER FIVE

By Design

It is a process of unravelling all the ways we are conditioned to think about the places around us, and then creating our own ways, our own spaces. It is a tentative, lurching process, sometimes making us feel trapped by endless trivial matters, sometimes giving us feelings of great excitement and discovery. What we have learnt is how much there is to discover, and that it is possible to make spaces that respond to women's needs. If we can become more aware of how buildings we live and work in relate to how we live, then we can create buildings that work with women's struggle for liberation rather than against it.

Frances Bradshaw, 'Working with Women'

On 10 March 1995, during a Resource Group meeting about the design of Strachan House (the larger building of which Savard's is a part), the architects brought preliminary drawings, outlining rough ideas for the building's design. In the 'tour' of the first floor plans, the architect pointed to an area at the easternmost part of the building and heard some reactions:

ARCHITECT: This white area here – that's the area for the street survivors. There's nothing drawn yet, because we don't really have any ideas. We're still working on what it's going to be like, so it's left out at the moment. We are planning for it to be in that location.

SHEENA: We can go ahead with it. How do we make it so that if we do find out that we don't get the funding in a year or six months, or two years, or whatever years it is? We're going to have to convert that area into something else for health services if we get funding for that, or another unit. So if we build

Women Street Survivors Project under construction at the eastern end of Strachan House (photograph by Robert Burley/Design Archive)

it, we have to build it so that other people can utilize it, or that it can be used for some other space. Just to flag that [trailing off]...

MARGARET: It may be used by others. It may end up, because of the timing issues, it may end up, with all our good intentions ...

AMIE: However, we can't compromise the design, with the notion that others may be using this right at the outset.

MARGARET: What does it look like when she walks in the door? What in the physical space (design) would help make a difference in providing shelter for the women?

The first part of this chapter rivets attention on design questions about the Women Street Survivors Project: What does it look like when she walks in the door? What in the physical space (design) would help make a difference in providing shelter for the women? What design ideas would reflect the founding ideas about a low-demand high-support environment to help women street survivors *come inside*?

From the very beginning, it was unclear whether the Women Street Survivors Project would ever secure funding for operating costs. These very real constraints had to be set aside, however, during design and development meetings in order to 'move ahead.'

The latter part of this chapter asks: Who should come to work in the Women Street Survivors Project? What questions should be asked of new staff during their job interviews?

All these questions circled around the most basic of all interrogations – what spatial and social or institutional structures would support the needs of women street survivors? Boundaries and dichotomies permeated the discussions: privacy and publicness, inside and outside, safety and danger, structure and flexibility, trust and dependency.

Consultation Processes

The members of the Women Street Survivors Resource Group decided that having consultation processes with 'women who are fragmented, who lead fragmented lives,' as one member put it, would probably not offer much constructive feedback on what the project should look like. The 'target population' was those women who had not been able to access existing services. They debated whether or not to hold focus groups at other women's drop-ins or shelters in the city to get feedback on plans and solicit ideas for the project. One member spoke forcefully on this point: 'But those won't necessarily be the women we're trying to reach. A lot of the focus groups involve people who have a level of comfort, trust in groups, and want to be in that situation, and know about groups. I'm not sure the focus group is the way to go. Those are not the women that I think we will be housing. The women we will be housing are far more isolated and marginalized by everything. I don't think I could get Mary who's on the street to come to a focus group, but I can sit with her and talk.' Another added, 'We don't know. The women we would target have not been indoors for quite a number of years. The drop-ins may know them. They may be known. But they may *not* be. Some will. Some won't.'

One of the front-line workers related how some of the women she'd worked with were very suspicious. These women did not trust the 'government' and wanted nothing to do with facilities funded from public coffers. They preferred to maintain their independence, and would ask of shelter workers, 'Is this government-funded?' Quick jokes were followed by laughter at the meeting: 'No, it's a gift from God.' 'But she's not on talking terms with God.' 'Or maybe she is God!'

In a more serious vein, a member asked, 'How can we talk to the women we're targeting? How do you pose questions?' Another quipped, 'They all want a one-bedroom apartment when you ask, but then you can't get them to go into a one-bedroom!' Some women have difficulty sleeping within four walls and behind a closed door. They have been raped there. The room may be 'possessed.' The woman who sleeps sitting up all night in a chair, chooses the chair over a room. This highlights a key problem in many consultation processes – do what people 'say' and what people actually 'do' coincide?

The general consensus was that the outreach workers for the project should talk individually and directly with isolated women living on the street whom they knew and had developed some rapport with. They would then report back to the Resource Group. In addition, a three-hour community design session was also held 13 June 1995 with front-line staff from a number of the city's shelters and drop-ins for homeless women, staff of Homes First, municipal housing officials, and the architects for the project. There were twenty in attendance in all. Two questions were posed before that meeting so that everyone could prepare ahead.

'What are the reasons why women cannot be provided for or are asked to leave?'

Answers came in a flurry. Women hoard or fill up their living spaces. Many collect newspapers, and these represent a fire hazard. Food collects, rots, and smells. Some women are physically violent. Some are loud, disruptive, and scream at other women or staff. Women who have pets are asked to leave. Women take other people's belongings. Making women have baths or showers can present a barrier for some. Curfews are not respected. Women are asked to sleep at night but do not. Women are barred for the use of drugs or alcohol, and some are barred from particular shelters for very long periods because of their violent behaviour. One of the front-line staff suggested that they should do a survey of different hostels and find out their barring policies. Perhaps hostels should be lobbied to change some of their rules so women are given a better chance of obtaining shelter in the hostel system instead of having *nowhere to go*.

'What would you recommend in space, design, and rules and policies, etc.,
in order to provide housing for these women?'

There were suggestions about a pacing and screaming room and an
outdoor courtyard to accommodate someone who may wish to continue to sleep outside. What about a series of different spaces to accommodate those who refuse to sleep lying down in a bed? Some may
want to have a private room. Others may simply prefer to draw a curtain across an alcove, yet be within hearing of all that is going on.
Another may like to sleep by a window close to the street, so that she
can keep track of who is coming and going. Someone may want to
sleep close to the staff room because this feels safer.

Members of the group assumed that the women would come and go
at will – and with great frequency. Several in the group thought that
the women might treat the house as a drop-in. One design suggestion
was that women be able to leave from their individual rooms, through
doors opening directly to the outside. Someone else cautioned that
anyone could then come in, uninvited. The value of lockable storage
was also highlighted – for women who may not want to stay inside,
but would appreciate a safe place to leave their 'stuff.'

Someone suggested providing a variety of spaces for women to use
(for example, music room, television room, quiet space, phone room,
kitchen) – to give women a choice – together with a well-ventilated
smoking room. Another front-line worker suggested that the staff area
should not be right by the main door, so that there would be no feeling
of surveillance or expectation of contact or reporting.

Perhaps large sliding doors could open into a common area, so that
women could open their 'rooms' up completely or close them for more
privacy. Bathrooms (with bathtubs and showers) should have closed
doors and locks. Another suggestion was that perhaps there could be
an area with some mattresses on the floor. When the women were high
or drunk, they could 'crash' there and would not have to leave or feel
that they should leave.

Suggestions for program development highlighted that the women
feel demoralized by too many rules. There would need to be concentrated, intentional outreach to women living on the street. Women
should not have to give their names or produce identification – no
paperwork should be required for admitting. Some women do not
want to commit to a binding arrangement on paper where things have
to be signed. Instead of requiring the women to conform to rules for

safety reasons, adjust the building so that it is safe (that is, non-inflam-
mable beds, curtains, and flooring). Would meals be prepared? Perhaps there should be some kind of life skills program offered so that
women could prepare for other housing if they chose to move on.
What about time limits? Women should be welcome to return.

Several suggestions for staff included that they would have to
acknowledge women's needs for territory. They would also need to be
flexible about where women would sleep, and need to be flexible with
rules.

The Design

The Resource Group, including the project architects, prioritized the
many suggestions and came to a consensus about design decisions
over several meetings following the community design session. As one
of the members put it, 'There are a lot of things. We can't accommodate
all these things. We have to make some decisions.'

A communal kitchen and lounging area would welcome women as
they first came in the door. The staff room was just to the right of the
entrance, with a small storage area adjacent. A kitchen wall separated a
smaller, more private lounge area and sleeping nooks in the back,
while more nooks were also provided by the front lounge, closer to the
staff room. Two full washrooms together with a washing machine and
drier completed the amenities.

The idea of 'sleeping nooks' was also gradually formulated over the
course of several Resource Group meetings. These nooks were to be
plywood modules containing bed, drawers beneath, a curtain, and
shelves. The modules were designed so that they could be moved
about, so the women themselves could determine their placement. The
impetus was to support flexibility in use of the space and, at the same
time, a sense of ownership.

The design offered a choice of lounging areas and kitchen space for
residents to use, storage lockers, two bathrooms, and privatized alcove
spaces. The open concept of the nook was not, however, at all sound-
proof. Within the confines of 2,000 square feet, the staff room was
located immediately by the main entrance. A second emergency exit
led into the main building of Strachan House. The design did not
include a private sound-proof smaller space for private meetings (for
example, between staff and resident), separate bathroom area for staff,
nor a well-ventilated smoking area.

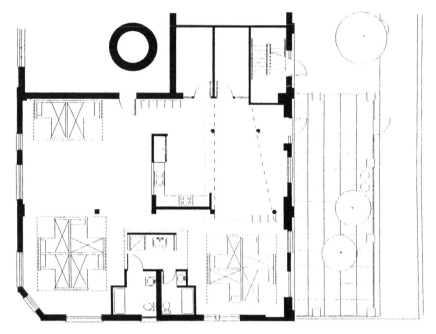

Floor Plan of Savard's (Levitt Goodman Architects)

Ideals and Recruitment

With the degree of care given to developing the vision of a safe haven and then designing it, the importance of ensuring that staff hired be sympathetic to the founding principles could not be underestimated. The job description posting began: 'The Women Street Survivors Project is an experimental alternative to the street or traditional hostel or shelter models. It has been designed to house those women whose life situation and personal needs deny them the option of safe housing. This project will be monitored and evaluated on an ongoing basis. The space will be provided and staffed to create an environment that can change and adapt to meet the needs of the resident as opposed to requiring the resident to conform to the rules of the shelter ... Due to the perceived nature of the target population only women will be hired.' The words *experimental, alternative, evaluation,* and *change* feature prominently in this description.

View of the kitchen from just inside the front door of Savard's (photograph by Robert Burley/Design Archive)

A series of questions were developed by the Resource Group to test applicants' depth of experience in working with homeless women. Case scenarios were also posed to probe applicants' understanding of conflict resolution and non-intervention, and their ability to deal with potentially violent incidents: 'What is your understanding of this position? What do you feel you could contribute to this position? This project is experiential in nature, and outcomes are unpredictable. We expect it to be flexible and evolve and change throughout the duration of the project. What is your comfort level with this kind of working

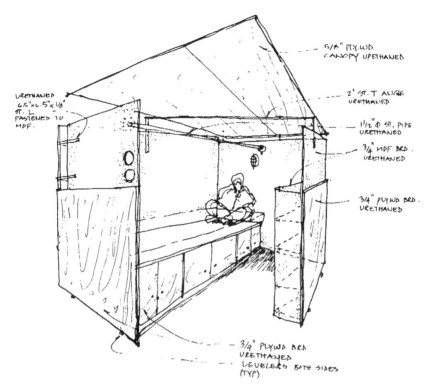

Sketch design for Savard's sleeping 'nook' (Levitt Goodman Architects)

environment? Can you draw on previous relevant experience you might share with us?'

Other interview questions follow, together with the kinds of answers the hiring committee was looking for (the committee was composed of Resource Group members and Homes First administrators):

Q: What are the issues that confront women who live on the streets?
A: Stigma. Violence. Poverty. Severe physical and mental health issues. Isolation. Hunger. Harassment.
Q: What are the issues involved in developing a relationship with a homeless woman?
A: It can be a slow process, involving potentially months for engagement. Building trust can be difficult, particularly if women's past experiences

Plywood sleeping 'nook' as it was built (photograph by Robert Burley/ Design Archive)

with the 'system' have been demanding. Multiple levels of issues (for example, addictions, abuse, etc.) may inhibit engagement.

Q: A particular woman, Mary, has been staying at the housing project for some time. You are the only staff Mary has made a connection with. Discuss some of the possible aspects of this relationship.

A: Positive: Mary is able to make connections with someone. Trusting one person may be the beginning of trusting and relating to others. Negative: You are not always there. There is the danger of fostering dependency.

Q: Susan has been staying at the project for the past 3 months. Previously she had been living on the street for 2 years, and this is the only information we

Two side-by-side sleeping berths at Savard's (photograph by Robert Burley/Design Archive)

have on her. Susan has no interaction with any of the other women or staff. She helps herself to food when no one else is around. What do you think your role is as a staff person?

A: Consistently make a point of acknowledging her on her terms. Make yourself available so she can access you. Allow Susan control of the pace of the relationship. Be aware of non-verbal communication.

Q: You're working night shifts, it's 2 a.m., and Anne begins screaming. Everyone's sleep has been disrupted, and the other women are being affected. What would you do?

A: Try to find out why she's screaming – directly from her or another woman.

Sleeping berth at Savard's. Pictures of household furnishings from a catalogue are carefully cut out and arranged on this resident's bed. Baby clothes together with a rag doll complete the 'installation.' (photograph by Robert Burley/ Design Archive)

Listen to find out what it is she is trying to communicate. Attempt to engage in verbal communication. Problem-solve with other staff and residents. Offer alternatives, for example, cup of tea, music, walk with her, invite her into office, offer her a bath, television, cigarette. Log the incident.

Q: Two women are yelling at each other. One insists she witnessed the other going through her belongings. The other denies it. What would you do?

A: Separate them, and allow each of them to tell her story. Negotiate ground rules so that each woman's story can be heard. Assess for safety. Offer options to deal with the situation. Gather information.

Q: What is your understanding of boundary issues in this type of work? What do you do to address them?

A: I have to separate the resident woman's issues from my own issues. Recognize that personal life needs to be separated from work life. There is danger of creating co-dependencies. Develop outside interests. Have a personal support system in and outside work. Be aware of boundary issues, and talk about them with co-workers.

Q: From your work and life experiences, what do you think the issues might be around safety for staff? And for the women?

A: Safety issues for staff and for residents will be linked – physical violence, fire, health and hygiene issues. Residents may mistrust other people (staff and other residents). Understand that perceptions of safety are determined by the individual. Expectations and rules need to be clear. There needs to be consistency in how women are treated. Emergency response plans need to be in place. There should be no single staffing, and supportive staffing group and management are important.

The questions delved into complex issues around trust and dependency, letting control of the pace of interactions rest with the women themselves, recognizing different forms of communication (for example, verbal and non-verbal), skills around mediation and negotiation, consistency in dealings with the women, and clearly establishing boundaries between work life and personal life.

What is *not* asked in the questions, however, can be as interesting as what is asked. The largest part of the questions queried applicants' responses to situations in which they had to respond as individuals to homeless women's behaviours. Very few questions actively addressed relations between members of the staff or between staff, administrators, and management. A number of case scenarios focusing on these relationships could also have been posed.

The ten women who were hired brought collectively over a hundred years of experience in social service agencies serving homeless women, as they joked at one of the earliest staff meetings. Some staff had young children. Some were attending graduate school part-time, or were working at two jobs to make ends meet. Some were single mothers, some lived with their lesbian partners and shared child-rearing. Several of the staff brought extensive training in substance addictions treatment and HIV–AIDS prevention, and mental health issues. One of the staff was trained as a psychiatric nurse.

Two of those hired were Aboriginal. For the most part, other staff were Caucasian. One of the staff interviewed spoke about her discomfort with what she called the apparent 'lack of colour' in the staffing group:

> I thought about that the minute I walked in, and saw everybody. I spoke with a couple of other staff. Many of us were very upset, and didn't know what to do. I can remember the first day sitting and thinking, I have to do something. I have to say something. But who do I go to? Who do I say it to? It's a new job, I don't want to cause too many vibes, but because of employment equity principles, and many jobs being allocated to women of colour and lesbian women, that's one of the reasons I was very surprised I got the job. I expected to be the only, or maybe one of two white women in the group. I don't have a problem with employment equity principles at all, so I really expected I'd be in the minority. So I was shocked, and I was disturbed by it.

Several of the staff had worked together previously for a number of years at another Toronto shelter for women, in fact, and knew each other very well already. In the drive to build a staffing team and open the project as quickly as possible, allegations around exclusionary practices during hiring only surfaced and began to be addressed by the Homes First Society after the project was in operation. One of the full-time staff at Savard's commented during an interview: 'I think the issue about the racism was so obvious. There were two Native women hired, but not even one black person was hired. When we know that there's a lot of black street women – never mind other women of colour – not one was hired on staff? To me, that was a big, big insult to the people who are living at Savard's.'

Conclusion

This chapter has concentrated on design ideas proposed for Savard's and some of the strategies for recruiting staff – ideas all fashioned to help women street survivors 'come inside.' Spatial flexibility, choice, and sense of ownership for homeless women were emphasized in the design. There were requirements that staff be flexible, active, and creative in their intervention and non-intervention skills, consistent in working with the women, and willing to let them control the pace of interactions. Moreover, there were to be no expectations of the women to change, and the project was an evolving one.

On 7 January 1997, the newly hired staff were brainstorming on what to name the new facility. The Women Street Survivors Project sounded too institutional. Ideas were jettisoned: something with the Wellington Street address in it. Name it after a private or corporate donor. 'Hope Haven,' 'Everywoman's Place.' 'Name it after the first woman who comes to live here?' It remained the Women Street Survivors Project for another couple of weeks. Then staff decided to name the project, Savard's, after Diane Savard.

Diane was born in 1956 in Alberta. Her family moved frequently, living in Canada, Australia and the U.S. As a child she was the victim of abuse, an issue she struggled with throughout her lifetime.

   She began to run away from home at an early age, dropped out of school and somewhere near her eighteenth birthday she ended up on the streets of Toronto. For several years she was in and out of hostels and cheap rooming houses, in jail or on the street. But, wherever she went, Diane made an impression. She had the unerring ability to empathize with others, to listen and to convey a genuine caring alternating between creating crises of her own and sorting out those of others.

   She returned to school first to Contact for upgrading, and later to the George Brown Addictions Counselling Course. Her first job was at Nellie's as a summer student in a 'Summer Escape' program in the early 1980s. She went on to work at All Saints Women's Shelter (before it became Cornerstone), Margaret Frazer House, and finally the Gerstein Centre. Diane could connect to the residents like few others and helped many to feel that they too could make it. She was always known for speaking her mind. For her entire working life she devoted herself to working with homeless women and/or people people in crisis.

   She died in her sleep in the fall of 1993, of natural causes (from the Women Street Survivors Orientation Manual).

With the new complement of staff, freshly renovated facilities, pristine appliances, and cupboards well-stocked with food and cutlery, the Women Street Survivors Project opened to women the middle of January 1997.

Staff were charged with the task of implementing the vision of a safe haven where women would be allowed to come and go at will, staff would act as resources for the women when they indicated their readiness, and non-intervention was a keyword. While rules were few, violence was not to be condoned. Nor was this place to be like conventional shelters with time limits on length of stay. Instead, it was understood by those who developed the project to have the potential to be a 'home' for the women who came to live there. One of the staff hired spoke about her expectations:

> It sounded like an organization that was going to really make an attempt to deal with the whole issue of a process for women who are really, really homeless. The ad was good. It convinced me that it was what I wanted to do ... I was going to be a housing worker, so I knew that I would primarily be working and living for 12 hours in the house for 3 days a week with the women. I don't know what it will evolve into. I don't think it's going to be a job where we'll be doing a lot of groups or referrals. I don't have that sense of it. It's primarily focused on shelter, feeding and support – physical and emotional support. That's probably what my expectations are, and I think that's the part that attracts me to it. I think I see it as a basic 'being there,' 'being with.'

Another spoke about working at Savard's as an opportunity for 'making a difference':

> I don't like oppression in this world
> and I don't like inequality
> and I don't like racism
> and I don't like classism
> and I don't like sexism
> and I don't like homophobia,
> whatever you want to call it.
> I don't like the fact that people are disabled
> and have barriers put up left, right and centre ...
>
> I have to have ammunition to say, 'This is my fight.' So that's what it is. It's a fight for equality and it's a fight to get rid of all the oppression in the world. I don't believe that I can do that on my own, but I think I can make a difference and at this point, for me, that difference is working at this project.
>
> I believe if I can do that, I can hopefully empower and enrich, help women empower themselves. I can't empower them, but I think I can enrich the women that we service a little bit and give them the respect that they deserve.

A third suggested, 'I guess I see this project as assisting people to somehow find their own power, their own strength in making their own decisions. And the way I see that happening here is in a very non-interventionist way, really just letting things evolve at a very slow pace, according to how the women want to do things. Certainly in most of the shelters, women receive lots of referrals and other suggestions ... and that's not really what it's about. Maybe they just need a place to be and that's good enough, and then, if they want to take it a step further, they can do that in their own time.'

The following two chapters continue the story of Savard's after it opened. Chapter 6 takes the reader inside Savard's to experience daily rhythms of living and working in the house. Chapter 7 then explores changes in the operation of Savard's and how these relate to the original vision.

CHAPTER SIX

Come Inside

This chapter simulates one week's worth of entries written by Savard's staff in the daily logbook. It is summertime. Savard's has been open approximately a year and a half at the time of the entries. Notes for each day span two twelve-hour shifts. Names of staff are not recorded for each shift, as is usually done, in order not to deflect attention from the residents and their rhythms. While there are approximately ten full-time staff, relief staff also cover shifts on a fairly regular basis.

I have simulated the entries in order not to compromise confidentiality for residents or staff, and in accordance with research agreements with the Homes First Society. The notes remain faithful, however, to the substance and tone of Savard's original logbooks, and echo their length, content, and format.

In much the same spirit as Chapter 2 (which features some of my actual fieldnotes on doing street outreach with chronically homeless women), this chapter provides an alternative and ethnographically immediate format for apprehending the daily cyclical rhythms of life at Savard's. Following the lead of Chapter 2, this chapter grants access to material that is relatively more 'raw' in character – yet strongly framed by the analysis of issues in Chapters 4, 5, and 7.

Savard's own daily logbook entries can be read as a genre of 'fieldnotes,' conscientiously recorded on a regular basis by the staff. They represent a tremendous collection of data susceptible to analysis, yet within limits. The notes are clearly framed by agency conventions and to set purposes of surveillance. They represent a record of organizational accountability, and are a vehicle for communicating to full-time and occasional relief staff issues that may require follow-up.

The following Homes First memo instructed all staff (full-time and relief) to clarify their log entries. 'Log notes should include all concerns that may have arisen throughout your shift, any and all disclosures, issues or problems arising through your shift, any health issues, any conflict or expression of aggression, any and all changes in behaviour, any administrative or maintenance concerns, directions or requests.'

The following are Savard's Rules to live by.

All our records could become court documents via subpoenas, etc. A court could determine all our records (i.e., logbook, to do book, etc.) are extensions of a client's personal file, and therefore a client could be granted access to all records.

Good records should state what you saw, what you did, and why. This allows for the recreation of what happened and the subsequent steps taken, as well as continuity of service.

The more out of the ordinary or untraditional a situation is or the more vulnerable or difficult the client is, the greater the need for extensive details in the records.

All statements should be objective, particularly those relating to drug and alcohol use, sexual activities, mental competency, or other sensitive matters (i.e., comments such as, so-and-so was wacked out on crack are not appropriate).

All records must be free of judgement or malice, such as derogatory comments or jokes about clients, expressions of personal frustration or negative feelings (i.e., so-and-so is a pain in the ass).

Entries should be made in chronological order.

Subsequent alterations or additions should be made openly, with the original entry left intact and legible.

Any corrections should be initialled, signed, and dated.

The author should sign the record.

The record should be made in dark ink and legible.

Records should be complete, as any omissions will likely be interpreted negatively.

The author should limit the records to issues that are relevant to the client's care/treatment.

Items that are relevant should not be omitted simply because they are embarrassing or uncomplimentary (for example, so-and-so has not had a bath in a week and is omitting [sic] a strong urine odour).

Information should be recorded contemporaneously – when the event occurs or as soon as possible thereafter.

As texts, the original logbook entries cannot be read uncritically, therefore. Depending on the writer and the circumstances, the entries may be cursory at times or reflective. Even when residents' experiences or thoughts feature in the logbook, they are mediated by the perspectives and interpretations of individual staff at Savard's (and in this book, by my own writing).

The simulated entries evidence a range of issues related to individual women's patterns of coming and going; environment and behaviour issues; resident's interactions and relationships; interactions between staff and residents, together with relationships between residents, and their families and friends. General policy and organizational issues at Savard's and the Homes First Society, and relationships between Savard's and its immediate neighbour, Strachan House (another Homes First housing project for chronically homeless women and men) also feature in the entries. Insights about Savard's in relation to its surrounding neighbourhood, other social service agencies, and municipal responses to homelessness in Toronto, can also be read through the entries.

The notes speak about a range of duties associated with being a 'Community Housing Worker': ensure a safe environment (physical space); ensure a healthy environment (in terms of physical and mental health); advocate on behalf of residents to outreach workers, social welfare and Family Benefits Assistance workers, and medical personnel; practise harm reduction[1] (for example, address safety issues, supplying condoms, encouraging proper disposal of needles, providing education to individual women); manage and maintain daily operations at Savard's; provide First Aid and CPR as required; administer petty cash, per diems and a personal needs allowance; facilitate communications between residents, staff, families, outreach workers, and other service providers; mediate conflicts between residents and crisis intervention; support and encourage women in their short-term and long-term goals; prepare and provide food; assist with referrals; maintain the daily logbooks; review residents' current status and situations regularly; provide basic personal needs (for example, clothing, health products); keep the house clean on an ongoing basis; provide informal and supportive counselling when needed, check up on women when they are outside Savard's; and search for other housing with and for women.

LOGBOOK

Monday, 9 am – 9 pm

To All Staff and Relief: We've just received additional notes re. record keeping from head office. Please read before next staff meeting!

   Leah returned around 5 pm, and was greeted warmly by the other women. She went out after supper, then returned about an hour later, then went out again.

   Sandy came home in time for lunch. Changed her clothes and went back out mid-afternoon.

   Ursula. Behaviour is different than what I see of her typically – considerably less polite than Ursula usually is, and aggressive towards Marcy, alternating between complimenting Marcy's physical features and then insulting them. When Marcy stood up for herself, Ursula raised her voice and argued back. Staff managed to contain and de-escalate the situation pretty quickly. Both were reminded that abusive language is not tolerated at Savard's. Ursula took her evening meds.

   Claire in all day. Watched a bit of TV in the afternoon, otherwise stayed in her nook.

   Simone. Rochelle from HOP [Hostel Outreach] called to say that Simone should be coming back to Savard's tomorrow. Simone has looked at some boarding homes and found nothing to her liking. Rochelle has requested that Simone's medication be kept in the office because there is the possibility of theft if the meds are left in her nook. Strong hallucinogenic meds – good street value. They are to be taken 2 times a day. Simone is willing to take meds and has gotten into a routine of doing it. Simone called to say hi & that she will be here tomorrow morning (has 1 pm appointment at HOP office).

   Maria. In all day, relatively good spirits. Took several naps. Cleaned her nook. Had a bath, and changed into clean clothes. Asking for smokes constantly. Went out around 4 pm.

   Martha. Very much in need of a bath. I tried convincing her to take one (unsuccessful). Went out shopping and came back with lots of stuff so she didn't eat dinner.

   Marcy was part of a brief altercation with Ursula, but situation was diffused pretty quickly by staff. Marcy had her hair nicely done by staff (Fran) today. Seemed very happy with the job.

Teresa. In all day. Cleaned up whole kitchen after lunch. Made her own supper, because she said she does not like chicken. In good spirits. Watched TV in the evening.

Sherry called to say she won't be coming back until tomorrow.

Carrie. Blair Connelly, a caseworker from Bridgewater, called. Saying that Carrie was with him & was claiming that she was kicked out of Savard's & now homeless. He had experience with her in the past so was calling to check her status. I told him that Carrie was not kicked out. It was her choice to leave, several months ago. She is supposed to be at another women's housing project, and from there, we have no knowledge. Told him she had ex-resident status and could come anytime. Gave him Kathy Clark's telephone # & told him to speak with her regarding Carrie.

Someone urinated on the flowered couch. I took off the cushion covers & washed them though there still are urine spills on the couch base.

9 pm – 9 am

Leah. Street Haven called to report that Leah was there & apparently looking unwell. Street Haven staff said (at 6 pm) that they'd encourage Leah to return here soon, but at time of writing (8:45 pm) we have yet to see her. (Hope she's all right.) Hospital called about 9:30 pm to inform us that Leah was there & that they will be sending her back by cab (they paid the fare). She got home shortly after, looking quite emaciated & in pain. She did eat sóme food at around 10 pm. Lots of laughing, overly affectionate touching, unable to follow a thought. Went to bed about midnight. Woke up and screamed due to blister on her foot at around 1:00 – it was causing her a lot of pain. Finally went back to bed at 1:30. Added 'Leah's declining health' as a possible staff meeting agenda item.

Martha in all night. Quite happy with bargains she found while shopping. Was wearing her new slippers.

Sandy home all evening – out at around midnight – did not return as of yet.

Ursula was up most of the night. Plans to go panhandling later on in the day. Told me I should watch out because my 'ex-husband' was following me and wanted to strangle me. Was chatting with Teresa. Got into a big argument with Marcy – see below.

Maria. Upon returning to Savard's around 5:30 pm, Maria entered the facility engaged in self-talk (was speaking incoherently about lesbians; didn't talk with anyone or visibly disturb them). Minutes later she was singing, at times rather loudly; nobody complained about the high decibel, even though 3 of the women were watching TV at the time. When I encouraged Maria to join us for supper, she told me to 'F off'. I reminded Maria that I don't appreciate profane language, and that it's not tolerated here. She made no further comment; didn't come to supper table. I found an ashtray in her nook, on the floor. Could staff remind her (again) not to smoke in her nook. Up until 4:30 am – restless, out in rain & bare feet for about 1 hr. Returned with cigarettes. Then went to her nook.

Marcy. Got back around midnight. Had a bath and went back out to work around 1 am. When she came back in, I noticed open sores on her legs. She got into an argument with Ursula, accusing her of stealing her cigarettes. Ursula vehemently denied it, blaming Maria instead. Marcy was extremely upset and began to shout that she didn't want her name said. Stated that Ursula had called Marcy 'an old hag' (staff didn't hear this) which spurred Marcy to tell Ursula to 'F off'. Upon confrontation by staff, Marcy (again) claimed that staff 'always sides with everyone else' (i.e., & not with Marcy). Marcy was (again) reminded that this is not the case. The situation de-escalated rather quickly. Ursula promised not to go into Marcy's nook.

Teresa was watching TV on and off. Talked either to herself or Simone about shopping for clothes until about 2:30 am. Reiterated her concern that Ursula might need to be in the hospital at this time; was reminded that staff monitor all behaviours and concerns. Retired to her nook, then got up saying she had difficulty sleeping, asked for food and finally went to sleep on the couch in the living room.

Claire was growling to herself, but then quieted down. Woke up once and ate but went back to sleep after making some tea in the kitchen.

Simone went out this morning for a while, had a quiet day. She and Ursula had a good long chat, but then Simone came to supper shivering, chills. Said she wasn't feeling very well. She threw up after supper. A gentleman friend came to see her at the door after dinner. Staff told him that she was sick, and asked him to leave a message for her. He insisted that he wanted to speak with her personally. Simone, already in her night-gown, spoke with him at the door briefly. We asked if she was okay as she passed by the office. Simone said she was fine. It wasn't our place to pose any further questions. Later she seemed to be feeling a bit better, and was chatting with Teresa.

Sherry. No contact.

Tuesday, 9 am – 9 pm

Ordered 2 buckets of laundry detergent because we're totally out. They can't deliver today but will tomorrow. They will pick up the empty buckets and credit them to our account. They're in the office instead of by the door so they don't disappear.

Fran, the nurse, dropped by today. She had a short visit with the house and will come back tomorrow because she didn't want to disturb the women as most were sleeping or quietly talking with each other. She didn't want to disrupt the energy that was going on. I think this is quite respectful of her.

Martha went out smelling very much like urine. It was suggested to her to bathe but she didn't. She came back around dinner time. Did not eat her dinner. Set aside some supper for her in the fridge in case she wanted to eat a little later.

Sherry checked her blood sugar level this morning. It's very high. She told me she will take her meds today. Sherry went out in the afternoon and has not returned yet.

Sandy out all shift, no contact.

Simone had a quiet day. Still not feeling well. Watched TV with Teresa. Told staff that she gets lonely at Savard's. Said she wished she could 'just talk' with people here. She mentioned, in non-judgmental tone, that Ursula can be difficult to talk with at times, and that Simone finds it hard to connect with others. I encouraged her to ask the staff here to chat with her when we're not obviously busy – emphasized to her that I didn't know of a single staff member who doesn't like her. In fact, I stressed, she is very well-liked, and I believe many staff would welcome a little chat with Simone during quiet times of the shifts. I also encouraged her to make use of close-by community centres, drop-ins – for social contact & maybe some fun, leisure activities. Gave her addresses & phone numbers. Encouraged her to explore such 'outside' agencies, one little step at a time. A friend then picked her up, and this picked up her mood a little. Seems terribly lonely.

Leah slept all day.

Maria. Simone was telling Maria to have a bath because Maria smells bad. Maria said no, she would bathe when she feels like it. When told by staff (Christine) that she could not have a cigarette, she started to call Christine a stinking monkey and a 'f' nigger. Christine then asked her to stop repeating this, but she kept on. We decided to time her out for 4 hours. She is due back at 10 pm. She came back, however, around

7:30 pm, and asked for bus tickets, and she got 1 ticket.

Marcy slept most of the morning. In okay mood – socialized a bit with other women. Had a long talk with me about HIV-AIDS. I went over info on symptoms which may appear in women. The conversation revolved around other people (friends & family) rather than concerns for herself.

Teresa washed the entire floor this afternoon. Then read the newspaper, was chatting with the others, and watched some TV with Simone.

Ursula was in & out for a good part of the day. Asking for cigarettes. Came to the office every 10 minutes to ask for something in the morning. Has slowed down since Rochelle (HOP) came and brought her a carton of smokes. She was given 1 pack & within 1/2 hr. she was back asking for more. Pls. do not give her full packs of smokes. She either gives them away or they are taken from her & she's back in the position she was 20 minutes before → no smokes & hitting everyone up. She's quite delusional – thinks she's pregnant. Doris, the nurse, came by to see Ursula today, but 'U' was not interested in speaking to her.

Claire. It was Claire's birthday today, and staff made a birthday cake for her (chocolate – chocolate with mocca icing!). Everyone sang 'Happy Birthday' after supper, and shared the cake. Claire seemed quite pleased.

Lisa phoned from StreetCity re. Gertrude Cranbrook. They are looking for a space for her. Please contact StreetCity if we have a space avail. in the next few weeks.

9:00 pm – 9:00 am

To all staff & relief:
When making changes to the schedule please *do not use arrows*. Pls. white out names & *write* in the switch! After 10 people do this in one week, the schedule becomes illegible. Thanks.

Maria came in about 1 am, and went straight to bed, after making some tea in the kitchen. Got up in the middle of the night and turned all the house lights on and made herself something to eat. She asked me if I would come out and have a cigarette with her. She talked about how difficult it had been to learn a new language, and about having a nightmare tonight. It was about a friend of hers who had died in an accident. She had talked with me about this accident previously – when she just came to Savard's. I remember her telling me that the friend had died. It must have been quite a traumatic experience for her – she is still dreaming about it 20+ years later. Maria asked for her $10.00 allowance at 6:15 am, received the full amount and went out for coffee. Came back at 7:45 and returned to her nook to sleep.

Leah. Encouraged to stay in but left at about 11 pm.

Ursula ordered pizza with F. Smoked, watched TV, and hung out in the house with others. Went to bed by midnight. Up early asking for smokes. Took morning meds, went to the store with F. and got smokes. Good spirits. Then went out again.

Sherry slept.

Teresa slept, woke up early in the morning at 6:30 am. Went out to have breakfast with a friend at 8:00 am.

Marcy. In & out, many showers in between, until 4:45 – then slept.

Simone was in all night, and ordered pizza with Ursula. Had a long talk with me in the office about wanting to return to university and her disappointment when she discovered she owes them lots of money and OSAP [Ontario Student Assistance Program] (she did not officially cancel classes during the time she got sick). Will try to talk to V. about re-negotiating $ with the college and OSAP. We discussed how she felt about being diagnosed with psychiatric problems & their possible implications. She talked about events which have taken place in the last 5 yrs., various losses, challenges, barriers to building her life back up. Talked about current feelings of being lost & overwhelmed at times.

Martha. In excellent spirits. Chatted at length about the CNE [Canadian National Exhibition], Ontario Place, Imax films, and other favourite entertainments.

Sandy. No contact.

Claire. In her nook all night, got up briefly during the evening to make a snack. Staff heard her throwing up in the sink beside the washing machine, asked her if she was okay. She said that she was fine and proceeded to clean up after herself. She went to bed shortly after.

Wednesday, 9 am – 9 pm

The day started out very quiet, until Marcy came home around 11 am. Slept for a while, then woke up in a rage.

Wanda, Fran, and Sally did a wonderful job cleaning under the nooks. Unheard of living and dead objects, etc. found under nooks ... need I say more ... The construction crew will return tomorrow to fix new beds. Also 'new' (well, old) furniture – all vinyl. Other soggy, pissed on furniture thrown out – hooray! Lot of donations came in – women have gone through most of it already.

Simone. Around noon said her locker key was stolen from her jeans pocket. Her locker was open and her purse was missing. Other women in the house said they saw Marcy snooping around Simone's nook. I helped Simone to look, just in case she lost it somewhere in the house – no luck. Staff talked with Marcy, but she denied any responsibility. Then I remembered Marcy taking out the garbage this morning. Simone and I went to check the dumpster, went through the garbage, and in one of the bags we found her handbag but her money was gone.

Maria was very quiet and pleasant today, although Marcy's screaming woke her up. Even serenaded staff with an old lullaby. Has a lovely voice! Went out after supper which she seemed to enjoy very much.

Ursula. In hospital. Called twice from the hospital. Spoke with staff, Simone, and had been hoping to also speak with Leah. Sounded subdued and rather happy. Told me that she's not sure when she'll be returning to Savard's because she 'waited too long for her injection' (her words). Says 'hello' to all. Then we got a phone call from HOP that Ursula will be returning at noon tomorrow. They'll be coming with her.

Marcy was just going around picking a fight with everyone in the house, including staff. Saw Marcy taking out the garbage in the kitchen this morning but the bag was only half full. I told her I would do that, she said no, she put some stinky stuff in there. I found handbag in the same garbage. Marcy claims she always takes out the garbage, said she didn't do it. More follow-up.

In the afternoon Marcy called Hostel Operations to complain that we keep timing her out forcing her to prostitute for *us*, we put her on street, made her ill that is why she's so sick. We're prejudiced against her – 'I want this place investigated.' She also started swearing at me because she came into the kitchen dressed in just a sheet & I told her this was not sanitary around food.

Teresa. No contact.

Martha. Came to talk. Is feeling very controlled by nurses, doctors, meds. Wants to have the nurse cancelled who gives her blood test, and does not want to continue with the doctor. Explained that we couldn't cancel her appts. with nurse at this moment. Asked her to talk with Lucie [HOP] and full-time staff about possibility of switching to a different doctor – although she thinks it may be drs. in general, willing to try a diff. one. Feels very strongly about the blood tests – connects having them with her illness and subsequent diet controls. If no blood test, therefore no illness and no need to control. Without her treats she feels that she'll starve. Tried to explain seriousness of illness and that meds have to be monitored, but feeling controlled a big issue. She went out shopping today to the mall.

Claire. In nook for most of the day. Came out just before dinner time to observe the preparations from living room. Had dinner at table with the house. Great! After dinner went to watch TV with others. Went out at 8:30.

Sherry. No contact.

Leah. Had a phone call from Lucie [HOP]. Leah's in jail. Will update us.

Sandy came back today & went into a cleaning frenzy. Busy doing everybody's laundry. Re-arranged all the things in the kitchen cupboards. We had a long talk about her current & ongoing frustration & sadness about where her life is & the various events which led her there (she was very weepy). She talked of difficulty asking for help and now she's trying. I put a positive spin on things by pointing out many positive changes over the last couple of years. She left about 4 pm and has not been seen since.

Annie from the City dropped by to say Hi, and donated a coat, a painting & a big soup pot.

More info from Marsha about Shalom House. Offers community kitchen and social activities for women with mental health issues. May be appropriate for some of Savard's women. Also Phoenix provides housing for women – this may be a good lead for Teresa or Sherry?

9:00 pm - 9:00 am

Sandy came in the evening with a cab driver who was asking staff to cover the $$ for the drive Sandy got from Hamilton to Toronto. Apparently this is a routine for Sandy to not have cash for cabs. Staff insisted that it's Sandy's responsibility to pay, although Sandy didn't seem to agree. The driver called police, but they couldn't charge Sandy because she has a mental illness, and therefore not held responsible for setting up the driver. After a long conversation, cops decided to give Sandy the opportunity to pay by Friday – if she doesn't, police could lay charges. So, please remind her to pay Friday. After this episode, Sandy went into the house and slept.

Marcy in & out until about midnight. Noticed that she was using a plunger in the toilet. Needles were thrown inside the toilet. I spoke with her & the consequences of using in the house. I am afraid she was not registering what I have said – I've told her that she can use a sharps disposable container as it is very expensive to fix the washroom. I've also indicated that she was going to have to stay outside as she has violated Savard's policies re. using drugs in-house. She was told that she is not allowed to lock herself in the washroom as she needs to share with nine other women in the house.

We brought her in the office & we repeated what was said earlier. We decided that she should stay in as she is not too coherent & will be very unsafe for Marcy to stay outside. Therefore, she will be in tonight followed by a conversation tomorrow.

Martha sleeping all night.

Maria in & out of the house throughout the night. Maria received 2 bus tickets today instead of 1, therefore she should get a single ticket tomorrow.

Teresa. Returned from a day's outing with a friend at 8:15 pm. Was in a cheerful mood, but then had an upsetting moment with Ursula. Teresa strongly criticized Ursula for being at Savard's. She even suggested she should go to Queen Mental Health Centre where there are all kinds of recreational activities – staff intervened, suggested Teresa to have some compassion & understanding toward Ursula.

Simone was out with her sister until about 10 pm, then returned, watched the news.

Ursula kept staff on their toes all night. Kept coming for smokes all through the night. Even though she was told quite clearly that at 3:30 am she would not be given any more of her cigarettes from the drawer after these last 2. Then she came back at 4:00 am, 4:30, 5:00, 5:30, 5:40 for a cigarette. Banging on office door & ringing doorbell were the ploys used. She did not want to hear staff telling her that her behaviour was totally inappropriate, she's disturbing others in the house by not lowering her voice. She completely does not hear anything that is presented to her. She smoked 1/2 a pack from 11 pm to 3:30 and only has 1/2 pack left.

Leah. In jail.

Claire came home at 11 pm. Didn't talk much, went straight to her nook.

Sherry. Out.

Large toilet was still plugged this morning (see above). I think we need to phone the plumber.

Thursday, 9 am – 9 pm

1/2 hr. into the shift & 1. The phone is busted. 2. Ursula is defecating in garbage can. 3. Teresa is screaming at Ursula for eating her *cat food*?

Ursula is defecating into the wastebasket. I took her for a walk to get a donut (house quiet), she thinks voices are coming from the computer, almost walked in front of a car on way back . At 2 pm – a knock at the door, a neighbour (male) passing by said Ursula was just on the road, took off her clothes, and peed on the road, I left a message for Rochelle [HOP]. Hopefully she will call early in am. Ursula is being picked on a lot too – Teresa is blaming her automatically for a lot. Sleeping at 7 pm. Evening meds not yet taken.

Sherry cleaned her nook and got a 2nd mattress as she doesn't like being close to the floor. Went to Coffee Time and got 6 donuts + 2 hot chocolates and pop – I reminded her of their high sugar level.

Maria. In all day. Personal hygiene seems to be [↓↓]. Refused all suggestions & encouragement to take a bath. She said, 'I can take care of *myself. You* look after yourself.'

Simone concerned re. baby being taken into custody – worried that if she had another child it would automatically be taken from her. Offered reassurance. Also worried about her fate if Savard's ever closes. Reassured her and explained that Savard's (as far as we know) was not closing down and even if this happens, women will not be sent to the streets, but alternative housing will be found for them. Simone told me that Marcy took $15.00 plus some change from her purse. Simone was paranoid that someone would let Marcy in. I assured Simone that we had made arrangements for Marcy to stay at another shelter, and that she will not be returning to Savard's until Friday at 5 pm. We talked about what to do when she saw Marcy. I told her, Marcy probably will not hurt her because then Marcy's housing would be in jeopardy. Seemed okay with our talk. Encouraged her to get some sleep. She retired to her nook for the night, settled about 12 am.

Marcy called from jail (x2) – worried her ex-husband is 'sicking' the cops on her – I explained cops were harassing and cracking down on all sex-trade workers, the homeless, the poor – she felt better after that. Thinks she should change locations. She phoned later to say that she had been released, and that she'd be home this evening sometime. Returned about 8 pm.

Sandy left about 10 in the morning, and has been out all day.

Teresa. In for a good part of the day, reading. Went out for a walk in the afternoon.

Claire. Kept to herself the entire day.

Leah. Jail.

Martha woke up in the morning covered in faeces. She told us it was chocolate! When we insisted that she wash up, she smeared the faeces all over the washing machine. Then we told her to clean up washing machine. Oh well, it went everywhere. Staff ended up cleaning up.

Carmen [ex-resident] phoned several times today. Spoke with staff about how lonely she was, and inquired if she could move back. Told her there was no beds available right now, but told her she's welcome to come for supper tonight or tomorrow, or to drop by.

A woman who said her names are Frances Carpenter and Angie Chartrand (age 43) called. She said Maria is her friend and told her she could live here. She will be here tomorrow at 10 am to talk to staff about this.

Lots of pre-cooked rice in fridge – please have fried rice tomorrow. Also, meat from Second Harvest in freezer – use quickly.

9:00 pm – 9:00 am

Ursula was talking to one of the plants early this morning (the plant's name was 'Bermuda'). She slept most of the night. Told staff this morning that she was fasting today as she refused to have something to eat when asked by staff. Staff, please monitor & try to encourage her to have her meds if she refuses.

Claire. Stayed in her nook all night.

Maria. In all night. Left for coffee around 8:30 am after making a couple of phone calls.

Sandy. No contact.

Leah. Jail.

Simone. In all evening. Retired early.

Martha. Out in the early part of the evening. Returned around 9 pm, then went to her nook.

Marcy went in & out about 3 times during the night. Took showers each time. She was in pretty good spirits. Slept until about 7 am, then got dressed, made some tea in the kitchen. Left around 8:30 for an appointment.

Teresa slept.

Sherry. No contact.

Friday, 9 am – 9 pm

Ursula is defecating in garbage (please read Thursday's log) – her rationale is she doesn't want to pollute the H_2O. I found a garbage bag & faeces in her locker & as well garbage can in large washroom full of faeces & urine. I am not sure but I don't feel so comfortable picking up faeces so regularly for Ursula. I also feel that she presents a health hazard at this point. I left another message for Cathy [HOP] explaining everything, she phoned back, and then dropped by just after lunch, to visit and talk with Ursula. She will contact Dr Crawford.

Sherry hung out, had shower, speaking to a lot of people on the phone. Then left for most of the day.

Simone is expecting a call re. housing today. Please get her for the phone call even if she is sleeping.

Claire got up & went to welfare all on her own this afternoon. Seemed in good spirits at dinner except Ursula took her plate of salad & Claire does love her salad.

Marcy. Gone for most of the day, then returned around 5 pm in time for supper.

Teresa. Out with a friend all day, returned in time to have supper with the house.

Leah. Mary [HOP] called. Update re. Leah. In court today – found 'not fit' to stand trial – has been ordered transferred to Queen Street [Mental Health Centre]. There she will get treatment + remain until she is fit to stand trial – Mary thinks they may keep her for up to 2 weeks. Mary thinks this might be positive for Leah + assist her in dealing with her issues. Will continue to update us.

Sandy. No contact.

Martha. Sleeping for a good part of the day. Bathed today, and tidied her nook a little, although the urine smell around her nook is quite strong.

Maria. No contact.

Carmen. Visited for supper, and quieted down considerably after I stated quite clearly that some manners at the table would be appreciated. (Marcy was telling me to give her, her fucking supper, that my f–g job is to f–g clean and f–g cook.) Carmen thanked me for a lovely dinner and a special treat. Watched a movie with the house, then returned back to her place.

Nancy from HOP phoned to say that they were hoping to bring by Larissa Chambers who has been living in the train station at Union Station. She's expressed interest in visiting Savard's to see what we're like. They'll phone again to confirm time.

Food order arrived.

Fruit/veggie order made.

I faxed info on Savard's to Rollie, Crisis Intervention, as she requested it.

Computer keyboard works – problem was computer was not plugged in!

Staff: I took my first stab at writing up the weekly menu – it's stapled to the rest of them. Please review it since this was my rookie effort! Thanks – Brigitte

9 pm - 9 am

Sandy arrived home at 10 pm. She came in extremely high & drunk – created chaos. She ate 3 plates of food & puttered around the kitchen until midnight then retired. At 1:30 am, I see that she's in Maria's nook sleeping (this is Sandy's old nook). (Maria isn't home yet.) At 2 am Sandy wakes for a cigarette and some pacing. I tell her not to sleep in Maria's nook. She doesn't – she goes to her new nook.

Simone watched TV in the evening, and talked on the phone with her mother briefly. Had a bath, then went to sleep for the night.

Leah. In hospital.

Maria returned home at 3 am – she approached her nook and noticed quite a few things have been re-arranged & placed down in her space. She wonders if she's in the right place. She thinks she isn't and tells me it's not her nook. I do quite a bit of reassuring. She returns to her nook at 4 am. 8 am – Maria's on the south room couch again – sleeping.

Claire. No contact.

Teresa. Delighted that Charlotte brought a camera so that we could take pictures of the cat. Smiling, chatted happily with both staff while we all chased the cat around, taking pictures. At around 10:00 pm, we were photographing by the smoking area, and Marcy began to complain & be abusive, since our (quiet, really) chatter & movements had roused Marcy. (See details under Marcy's name.) In between staff interventions to calm Marcy down, staff let Teresa assert herself & express her feelings & thoughts to Marcy, which Teresa did quite well. Good for her! Retired to her nook at 1:30 pm.

Marcy. Not impressed by the noise (see above) that roused her. Marcy complained that staff pick 'their favourites' among the residents; she also stated that we were all inconsiderate since we roused her (10:00 pm) inadvertently. Charlotte reminded her that it wasn't a terribly late hour, and that – rather – Marcy has disturbed the house on some occasions before this, when she returned late at night and was 'banging around.' Charlotte then asked Marcy for 5 minutes of quiet; Marcy had trouble granting this request & had to be reminded that if she couldn't give Savard's 5 minutes of peace, then Charlotte would give the house an hour of it by Marcy being 'timed out.' Marcy then began – thankfully, in a quiet way – for the rest of the period, to try to make staff feel guilty for this, saying 'I guess I should go out then & turn tricks.' She quieted down, but prepared to get ready to go out – left around 11:30 pm, saying that she's going out on the street where she's 'treated better by men than the women in here.' Marcy returned at 2 am, immediately removing her heels at the door – staff quietly thanked her for sharing this consideration. Marcy then, quite lucidly, apologized for her behaviour earlier. She that her behaviour was 'dumb' and 'silly', and that she regretted it. Then went to her nook & has been there ever since.

Ursula. Shat in front of Strachan House. Also stripped on King Street in front of staff. Cathy [HOP] came by & stated she thinks if Ursula's meds bumped up this behaviour will stop. Pharmacist said Dr approved increase & Ursula's meds bumped up. Please note when giving her the new increase, she started them on pm meds – so monitor behaviour for changes.

Martha. Out for Burger King. Had pm meds.

Sherry. No contact.

Shelley came by tonight. Told me that she's been sleeping on one of the grates downtown. I asked her if she was interested in returning to Savard's and she indicated she didn't like sleeping inside. Wanted to leave me $40 for the house cat to go to the vet. I convinced her to keep the $ + let me look into what the cat needs. She also needs a sleeping bag. I have called Strachan House – no sleeping bags there, but they've got those heavy quilts, so I will get her a quilt from next door.

Carmen (ex-resident) called 5 times this shift – profane, loud, abusive language. Staff quickly terminated these phone calls.

Saturday, 9 am – 9 pm

Ursula. Fairly pleasant mood, socialized + went out. Gave Sandy a big hug & kiss + said she loved her, when Sandy was crying (almost made *me* cry).

Simone. Quiet today and in a pleasant mood. She asked if we ranked people here according to ability & as such, judge when they should move out and wanted us to know she is as needy as anyone here – I assured her again that this is not the case. She said this had been bothering her for some time & so I encouraged her to come to us with any concerns/questions she has at any time & that we are not the ones who would ever put any pressure on her in this regard & only she knows when she's ready & again that she is very welcome here – Simone took her pm meds.

Marcy. Feeling quite sick, threw up a couple of times. Staff offered to call an ambulance for her. She was furious!

Maria. In and out during the day. Slept in the evening.

Teresa. In all day, made brownies in the afternoon for everyone.

Martha had to be reminded again today that she is not allowed food in her nook. (The amount of crumbs that were swept from there today ...) Please redirect her to kitchen table. Went out & came back with a box full of goodies.

Sandy. No contact.

Claire. Stayed in her nook all day. Came out briefly to get her supper, then returned to nook.

Sherry. No contact.

Leah. In hospital.

9:00 pm – 9:00 am

Relatively quiet shift. Like a proverbial morgue by 11 pm – everyone already off in their nooks. Only Marcy and Maria were somewhat rude, but even those moments were short-lived.

Maria. 'Dear ... ?' 'N-o-o-o. I don't have a spare cigarette!!!' Greg (from West End) is due here at 9 am with her smoke $$, and Maria has exhibited the patience of a boiling tea kettle over this. Up and down all night, in and out. Maria left a recorded message for Greg, reminding him to come at 9 am. Charmed me by telling me to f off when I declined her last request; was clearly advised that I didn't appreciate her language. On a positive note, has (really for the most part) been calm & pleasant.

Sherry. No contact.

Sandy. In jail.

Teresa. Chasing after the cat, who's enjoying the ceiling beams – what fun! In good, calm spirits. Watched TV with Marcy.

Ursula. Subdued, pleasant but appears pre-occupied and somewhat delusional. Cigarette after cigarette ... Otherwise, no concern.

Claire. Quiet & calm. No concerns this shift.

Simone. Her pleasant, sweet self. Minimal contact. Came for meds early this morning & I asked her if she'd still like us to dispense & record meds; in response, she said, 'It's up to you.' I gently corrected her: 'Actually, it's really up to *you*.' I note this because I think this is a positive sign – maybe more trusting.

Marcy. Has been (for the most part) relatively pleasant. Spent the evening doing laundry & watching TV with Teresa – in a mellow mood. Even (appropriately) laughed at herself, her clumsiness, when she accidentally shattered a glass – co-operative & helpful as staff swept up. Spent the entire night in the house! Only a bit cantankerous in the early morning about Maria 'constantly bumming smokes off of me' – situation was quickly addressed, Marcy calmed down right away, and was pleasant again. Wanted us to record that she gave Simone $20 yesterday in regard to theft from Simone's purse. She wrote her own note and signed it. She wants us to destroy the other note which states that she owes money to Simone. Staff informed Marcy that we will destroy the previous sheet about her debt once we verify this with Simone. Simone was out when Marcy came in to talk about this. Simone confirmed that she received $20.00 from Marcy. Marcy also needed assurance that the $50.00 she gave us yesterday will go towards the long distance telephone calls she made. Staff confirmed with her that the $50.00 was placed in a separate envelope in the petty cash box.

Leah. In hospital.

Martha. Did laundry this evening, and cleaned nook (neighbour still complaining of urine smells & stickiness). Went to sleep about 11 pm.

Carmen. Came over for dinner & watched a movie with the house. Finished her visit around 9:30 pm – pleasant spirits. Left without incident.

Sunday, 9 am – 9 pm

Martha. Pleasant mood today. Stayed in all day. Ate dinner with the house.

Leah. In hospital. Had a phone call from Leah in the afternoon. She was concerned that someone else may take her bed at Savard's. Reassured her that her things were safe, and that we would be keeping her bed for her. She asked to speak to Ursula, but Ursula was out at the time.

Maria. Kept trying to fool us into giving her $$. We were firm with *No*. She pissed on the couch & later wet herself again – seems oblivious to it.

Marcy did nothing but complain for the 1st half of the day, was spoken to sometimes for screaming & rude comments. She did express concern to staff that she thinks Teresa is going crazy because she keeps talking to herself in her nook all night. Staff replied that Teresa could be talking to the cat and that many women here talk to themselves at times. Marcy also managed to set Ursula off in a rage, which seemed to be what she wanted, 'cause she was good as gold after it.

Simone was out for the day with her family, and returned early in the evening. Seemed happy.

Sherry. No contact.

Night staff: If she does not return by midnight, please check hospital again. Her friend, Phyllis, phoned yesterday looking for her, which indicates she was not with her, as she usually is when she does not return to Savard's. She is not at the detention centre either.

Ursula. Pleasant and social for most of the day. Except when she reacted to Marcy's bitching. Ursula started to scream at her, telling her to f off & called her various names. I got U. to come outside for a smoke & she calmed down.

Sandy. In jail.

Teresa got annoyed with the ongoing arguments between Ursula & Marcy, and left to go for a walk.

Claire was in her nook all day, then went out at 7:00. Kept her supper in case she wanted to eat later.

9 pm - 9 am

Marcy was in for the evening, then went out at around 1:30 am. Returned about 4 a.m., still in a good mood. She brought staff coffee, went out at again at 5:45 am. She is thinking about going to the dentist in the near future so staff encouraged her with her decision. She is having problems with her teeth.

Teresa seemed to be lurking close by the door this evening around shift change, paying attention to what is being said in the office – staff should be careful. In all night.

Ursula. Oh boy!! This woman has not slept a bit – in transit, in & out all night. Took clothing with her – I've suggested that she stay in, but Ursula's psychotic episodes are quite annoying for everyone in the house.

Sherry called from the West General Hospital to say that she has been admitted there. When I asked her why, she told me that she felt suicidal, so she committed herself. She said she will be home on Monday.

Sandy. In jail.

Claire. Returned at 10 pm, ate the supper that had been kept for her, watched TV briefly, said good night, and went to her nook.

Simone. Slept all night.

Leah. Hospital.

Maria. Roaming in the house during night, then settled down.

Martha. In her nook all evening. Slept the whole night.

Monday, 9 am – 9 pm

Phyllis, Sherry's girlfriend, called in the morning trying to get information about Sherry. I told her to call the residents' phone. The residents' phone started to ring in less than 2 mins. Ursula picked it up, I heard her telling the person, 'Sherry is not here, Phyllis. Sherry is not here.' Ursula put down the phone and Phyllis was still on it, screaming a lot of abusive language and profanity. I told her I was staff and what she was doing was not okay She went on screaming. Staff hung up the phone, and left it off the hook for a while.

Martha went out to do some shopping – returned with a new sun hat. Went out again in the evening.

Maria. In a pleasant mood most of the day. Was given a clean change of clothes after she peed on the others – changed, then went out for a beer. Returned around 7 pm.

Sandy. Out of jail on bond conditions. She called & left message on voice mail to say she was fine. That she was just having a beer with a friend today, then she'd be home later this afternoon. She returned home in time for supper, and we made a cake with dinner to celebrate her return. Perhaps we all could celebrate with every woman as she returns home from the hospital or prison etc. after being away.

Questions were being asked about what happens when women are away from Savard's (i.e., if they're in jail or in the hospital – if they're coming back to Savard's. The staff reassured them that they were coming back and that we hold their beds because this was their home. Everyone seemed relieved about that.

Leah called from hospital – sounded in good spirits & said she'd bathed, done her hair nice & was eating lots of fruit. Asked for her HOP worker's phone #, which staff provided her with.

Simone. A peaceful day. Simone made a cake for everyone in the house!

Claire. Stayed in for the day. Sat listening to the radio. Did not speak with anyone, but stayed on for supper, then returned to nook.

Sherry. No contact.

Ursula. Got her morning meds. A little nervous after Phyllis abused her on the phone.

Marcy. Out all day – no contact.

Teresa washed clothes and cleaned nook in the morning, had lunch, then went out after lunch. Returned at 8:00 pm.

Camco came to fix the washing machine today. The repairman said that reason why the washing machine is leaking is because too much laundry detergent is being used. We should not use more than one cup of soap because the extra suds overflow and go underneath the machine. Please try to encourage all the women to use *1 Cup only*.

9 pm – 9 am

Martha returned about 9:30 and went straight to her nook for the night.

Teresa watched TV in the evening. Trying to quit smoking. Spent a lot of time knitting & socializing with others. Talked to herself in her nook until 1 am, then fell asleep. She got up at 5 am to feed the cat. Staff encouraged her to go back to sleep. She took the cat and went back to bed at 5:45 am. She continued talking to herself after going back to bed.

Sandy left the house briefly for a walk at 9:30, then returned about 10 pm, made some tea in the kitchen, then went to her nook. Slept all night.

Claire. In nook all night. There were some growling noises, words indecipherable. After a couple of hours these mostly subsided, pretty quiet for the rest of the night.

Sherry did not come home last night. Returned early morning 7 am. Came in intoxicated. We asked her to go to bed.

Simone. Slept all night.

Marcy returned at 10:30 pm. She went out & came back in a couple more times. Not a word from her or any commotion. Sleeping now.

Ursula was convinced I (Sharon) was visiting her in her dreams, that I stole her Bible, and we were competing for the same man. I did my best to reassure Ursula.

I forgot to note something that happened during the day shift yesterday. Since Teresa is trying to quit smoking and Ursula smokes a lot, Teresa asked her to take her cigarette outside (one of a handful of occasions). Ursula agreed to do this, but once – while she smoked outside – she asked Teresa, 'Is that too smoky for you? Is it too smoky? Is it?' The tone sounded taunting, and I firmly asked Ursula to respect Teresa's efforts at quitting. In response, Ursula said, 'Oh she quit? Oh.' Nothing more.

Maria. Up and down, in and out, all night. Broke the house record! In pleasant spirits, though, during minimal interaction she had with staff at 3:30 am. Maria spoke, again, about returning to her 'beautiful country' – stated she might go back as early as this weekend, on a one-way flight. Very nostalgic behaviour.

Leah. Hospital.

Tuesday, 9 am – 9 pm

After a fairly quiet night, we had a morning blow-up. Marcy was cranky this morning. Blaming staff for going on the street. Brought a bunch of needles [unused] and dumped in garbage. Sandy got involved in a shouting match. Teresa also came out and got frustrated. After telling Marcy that if didn't stop, she would be timed out, things de-escalated fairly quickly. Marcy called police to complain. Later explained that didn't use drugs, only keeps needles for memory of good times in past.

Sherry. Out in the afternoon. Spoke with staff about getting her SIN [social insurance no.], OHIP [Ontario Health Insurance Plan], and birth certificate. We did some work with her on this.

Claire was working on one of the crossword puzzles most of the afternoon. Seemed to enjoy the stew at supper. Watched TV with the others for 1 hour.

Simone. Out in the afternoon to spend evening with her family. She has her meds with her.

Martha. Quiet day. She & I cleaned her nook up. The nurse came &

met Martha (she'll be back next week). One thing to watch out for is that Maria has been dumping clothing, food & other stuff in Martha's nook – I asked Martha to inform staff when it happens.

Leah. In hospital.

Marcy. Out all day.

Ursula was quiet in the morning. At one point, I found her in Marcy's bed sleeping so woke her up and asked her to go to her own bed. After returning to her bed she continued her nap. She went down to Dundas Street, and apparently withdrew $70 from her account. She bought cleaning supplies for the house (these are in the office), then she said she gave away the rest of her money to strangers on Yonge Street. This is one of Ursula's better days. She was in very good spirits today. She did not bother staff every second for cigarettes even though she has lots of smokes that Rochelle from HOP brought her today.

Maria said that perhaps she will postpone her trip till next year when she is feeling better – 'Time heals.' And I agreed. Able to address quite a bit about her illness – talked about an accident and death of a friend who died as a result. She also approached me for Tylenol, saying that she thought she may have lice because her head is itchy. I was going to get her (*possibly*) to wash her hair but I cut my hand. Anyhow, when I approached her later on, asking her if I could wash her hair for her she cursed at me. Earlier I checked her hair and there are white things in it. She certainly needs to shampoo her hair with lice shampoo. Simone and Teresa are very nervous about catching lice. Teresa is upset that I didn't force Maria to wash her hair. Please get her to shampoo hair & comb. She went out about 8:30.

Sandy. Got involved in a brief altercation with Marcy that quickly subsided. Then went for a walk, and to do some gardening next door.

Teresa. She was fine and pleasant until she started complaining about Maria. She appears to be very worried about catching lice.

Clarice from Hostel Services was faxed a description of Savard's for their publication on services in the city.

A woman named Karen came + donated 3 bags of extra large clothing – she can donate more if we need it. She'll drop by next week again.

Nancy, HOP phoned to say that Larissa Chambers will be coming tomorrow at 10 am to visit Savard's. They're picking her up and will be coming with her (she's living at Union Station).

CHAPTER SEVEN

Natural Progression

Non-intervention shifts from shift to shift. It's like you decide when you come in the morning, 'How non-interventionist am I going to be?' Each person decides at that time – shift by shift, minute by minute. It was like the American Constitution ... the Founding Principles set down by the Founding Fathers (or the Founding Mothers). It was like they were never going to change. You'd think that we'd want to reflect on what had been learned, and think what could be better, what should change.

I think they had that big assumption that said, 'We don't get women long term. We'll get the drop-ins.' So they never said they would have a core group to work with. Their assumption always was that this core group would change. They would never see people on a continuous basis. And that's why I always refer to a natural progression. When, in fact, you see that didn't happen, and that women came to stay, then, of course, you have to stop and say, 'Okay, this changes things.' You can't operate with the same principles.

This chapter begins with the words of two Savard's front-line workers. The first was interviewed after the project had been open one and a half years. The second quotes another staff member, interviewed when the project had been open for almost three years. Keeping in mind, 'You can't operate with the same principles,' this chapter explores shifts in the operation of Savard's, as staff worked daily with the original vision – 'that we recognize is ragged around the edges, whose boundaries shift and change, and one that requires the vision and knowing of others to patch together' (Schneekloth 1994:302).

This chapter looks explicitly at the original decisions about what a safe haven should look like and how it should operate. How were these upheld during its first three years? Or how did they shift? What does 'safe haven' mean now? Of continued interest is the concept of non-intervention. The notion of needs of the one versus the needs of the many also echoes throughout this chapter. The framework of utopian pragmatics appreciates the grounded complexities of bringing ideas, programs, and projects to fruition, and for exploring their longitudinal evolution.

Juxtaposed are key insights from interviews with eight full-time staff and two relief staff (interviews conducted when Savard's had been open for approximately a year and a half), fieldnotes taken during staff meetings, orientation days, and visioning retreats, as well as insights gathered during site visits. Many of the women, both residents and staff, were highly articulate. I have intentionally foregrounded their narratives in this chapter to convey their depth of reflexivity, as well as their passions and uncertainties.

Discernible are tensions between original staff and those subsequently hired, as the original staff departed one by one. (Most of the original full-time staffing group had left by the end of 1998.) Many of those hired after the first year of operation (referred to as the second generation staff in this chapter) were drawn from the relief pool. There was also greater representation given to women of colour, as the Homes First Society took action on issues related to diversity and employment equity within the organization.

Remember the standards enshrined in the First Principles for the Women Street Survivors Project. (These were introduced at the end of Chapter 4.)

> This is a project that will evolve and change as the women involved teach, educate, and inform us about their strengths, abilities, issues, needs, wants and perspectives.
>
> The space will be an 'envelope' that will respond to the ways in which the women want to live or be in it. The space will 'fit' the women rather than the women 'fitting' into the space.
>
> No rules (other than what is necessary for health and safety) or treatment/program requirements will be placed on the women. There will be no expectations placed on the women to change. A flexible, non-judgmental, low-demand atmosphere and structure will be provided.
>
> The strengths, skills, and survival abilities of the women will be recog-

nized and respected. They will determine what, if any, supports, programs and services they want.

Enshrined in these principles are respect for questioning and openness to evolution and change. Within such parameters, 'natural progression' perhaps offers a fitting metaphor for understanding changes at Savard's. 'Natural' does not mean change necessarily happened easily or imperceptibly, however.

In what follows, several tensions are explored – ideas about Savard's as both hostel and home, funding uncertainties, and their impact upon both staff and residents, flexibility, and degrees of resident involvement in how Savard's operates. The latter half of the chapter attends to what dominated so many of the early visionary discussions – *non-intervention*.

Hostel or Home?

Chapter 4 highlighted the potential for Savard's to evolve as a permanent form of housing should the women living there want to remain. That potential for the permanent was in tension, however, with municipal and provincial funding mandates dictating that it be transitional only.

In early discussions, Women Street Survivors Resource Group members asked each other on a number of occasions: 'Is this project transitional housing, a hostel, or will it become a home for some women?' One had said: 'The money is coming from Hostel Services but it's not a hostel. It's not a hostel, but it is a hostel? It's permanent, but they can come back when they've left? We want it to evolve. How do we present, "This is your home. You can stay as long as you want"?'

The fluidity between the temporary and the permanent continues. A staff member interviewed when the project had been open for just less than a year reflected:

> One of the residents asked me, 'Is this a hostel or is this a home?' It's whatever she wants it to be. It can be your home or it can be a temporary place for you. Some of the rules are explained when they first come. We often explain timing-out to them, and we emphasize, we try to, that they won't be barred, so those basics are often explained when they come. The rest of the time it generally just comes up over conversations, over cigarettes, over the dinner table, or when something happens, more infor-

mally. I think most women get the message that they're not going to be barred, that this is different when they come in. I'd hate to have to present them with, these are the policies, these are the rules, this a piece of paper that explains it all. *That's not home.* Do you get that when *you* come in the door? ... I don't.

Another of the original staff members mused about the tensions associated with 'home' and her attempts to defuse potentially volatile situations:

Some nights, there have been bizarre evenings which are a bit like a Victorian novel, where Connie's embroidering, and someone else is colouring, and someone else is doing laundry. Couple of people playing cards. And we're all sitting around chatting, the music's playing, and sometimes we have classical music.

But then there's the whole dinner thing and we set the table. I don't do it now because I was finding that there were a lot of explosions at dinner. I think, because it recreated some kind of forced 'Leave It to Beaver' [a family television show] expectation around the dinner table, a sense of coming together as a family. I really got a sense that people were playing out roles from other places, and people were sitting, but they were very mechanical around dinner. There was very little table talk, aside from the clashes. What I try to do is stack the plates buffet-style, so that people can come along and get what they want and sit anywhere.

A second-generation staff member reflected on how ideas about 'home' intersected with a sense of ownership and changes in the general sleeping patterns of the women over two years:

When I see a woman at the very beginning, [she is saying] 'What do you mean? This is *not* my home. I had a home.' She's swearing at me, screaming at me. And then I see now, 'This is *my* home. What are you talking about? *I* sleep here.' Do you see the ownership – the shift? And the sleeping pattern – for about a year these women could not sleep at night, and now they all sleep at night. Three or four hours, but they do it. So, these are minor things. Slowly. And one woman who steals, and four of them sat with her. You were stealing our food, this is *our home*, what are you doing? You're giving it out there, to your men. And they were furious, and they really confronted her. 'It was my coffee.' 'No, it wasn't *yours*. It's *our* coffee.'

One of the residents during an informal conversation compared Savard's with where she had lived before. Amidst her questioning and frailties, she clearly appreciated what Savard's was trying to do: 'Why do I leave this place, when I know it's safe at night? I took off to my old boarding house for a couple of days. It has 35 rooms and a place in the basement for meals. It's much nicer here. Why do I leave? They try really hard here. This isn't a shelter. It's supposed to be a home, isn't it? I've got to make this my home. I shouldn't leave. Why am I scared?'

Funding

The expressed mission of the Homes First Society is to ensure afford-able and permanent housing for people who are homeless and have the fewest options in Canadian society. Government funding mandates privileging temporary, transitional housing, and a lack of appreciation of a model predicated on learning from homeless women themselves made it difficult for Savard's to obtain permanent core funding. One of Homes First Society administrators spoke about the tensions between the Homes First mission and provincial government funding man-dates: 'When it comes to our funding from government, the Ministry of Housing is the toughest nut to crack on the whole empowerment piece. That was never part of its agenda. We believe we need a fairly intense level of staffing and a fairly high level of funding, because the people we're housing are particularly hard to house. The government looks at it, and says, the empowerment piece doesn't mean anything to them. [They ask] to what extent do you need that high level of funding because of the nature of the people you have? So, we have a situation where our internal philosophy and the external validated philosophy are not the same thing.'

Before the Homes First Society actively began a fund-raising drive targeted to Savard's, staff were responsible for fund-raising in addition to their many other daily duties. Fund-raising for an expensive project, with operating costs in the vicinity of $600,000 per year was difficult.

One cold November afternoon in 1998, one of the Savard's staff described for me how she had told one of the women at 11 o'clock that morning: 'We've got to get this pail of shit and urine – pee and poop – out of here. It's not acceptable in terms of health. We have someone coming from the Ministry of Health to visit us, and this place has got to look good, or this could endanger our funding! This is your choice, if you want to pee in a pail, but you've got to realize these are the long-term implications – if you do this, then this may happen. We may have to take steps. It's up to you.' The nook was indeed cleaned up by 12 noon.

With no private space at Savard's, the meeting with the visitors from the Ministry of Health that day took place at the kitchen table. All the women were quiet in their nooks during the visit. Staff related how the visitors asked questions around crisis intervention, and it was extremely awkward to answer those kinds of questions within the hearing distance of all.

In discussions about fund-raising, Savard's staff, the Resource Group, and Homes First Administrators debated the merits of 'Plan A' which involved fund-raising for Savard's, and not making any changes in its operations. 'Plan B' called for cost-cutting measures. One Savard's front-line staff related the outcome of discussions during an interview: 'Plan B for Homes First administration has been cut hours. Or cut the time of day. Or cut staff. Or increase the number of women. Or charge rent. Finally, we all talked about that as a group, and we pointed out that it would change the nature of Savard's. It wouldn't be Savard's any more, if it weren't open all the time. It would be something else. And that would be the end of the research project. That would be the end of it. Then the discussion became disaster planning, in the event it closed.'

Savard's staff had worked on media outreach to bring the plight of homeless women in Toronto and Savard's funding uncertainties to public attention. Michele Landsberg (1997) wrote in the *Toronto Star* 'Where will homeless women go if new shelter dies?' and ended her article with: 'Savard's must finish its unique and hopeful research. The provincial Ministry of Health remains stubbornly silent – it has not responded to a grant proposal. Will one of those newly elected Toronto MPs bestir themselves? Will a chastened federal government finally listen, and save Savard's?'

To survive financially, Savard's was forced in late 1998 (at the behest of city officials) to increase the number of women living there from ten to fifteen. Two of the beds were designated as drop-in or emergency beds. Even with ten women, two staff (and during shift change, four staff), visiting medical personnel, and other visitors, Savard's 2,000 square feet had been more than filled already.

Core funding from the Ministry of Health in May 1999 was finally secured, but in order to gain such funding, partnerships with other agencies were required. The core funding dollars for the Savard's project were funnelled to the Homes First Society through an administrative association with Houselink Community Homes.[1] This administrative arrangement was necessary, as no Ministry of Health funds were being allocated to organizations that had not already received such funds in the past. All these externalities exerted their impact directly and indirectly on staff morale and affected whether Savard's ideals could be maintained.

With its change in status from being designated as a pilot project to enjoying more stable core funding, it also became apparent that more elaborate processes of accountability would now be required to accord with funding requirements (for example, proving the worth of the project through the numbers of women moving on to other forms of more conventional housing).

Management, Staff Morale, and Uncertainty

The Women Street Survivors Project was first developed by a group quite independent of the Homes First Society. Once the project opened, there were tensions between the vision developed by the initial Resource Group and Homes First general operating procedures and union agreements. The Resource Group and the newly hired staffing group self-identified as a collective embarking on an experimental project. Their consensus-building working philosophy distinguished it from all other Homes First Society projects. Staff were originally offered contracts for only three months, however, in accordance with available funding.

Funding uncertainties had a tremendous impact on those who actually came to live at Savard's, and on staff morale. Staff received their 'pink slips' (official notices about being laid off) more than once. By the end of two years, all the original staff had left, and the project relied increasingly on relief staff. A new generation of full-time staff was hired, and half of this new generation left within the following six months. The Ministry of Health was then concerned that Savard's staffing was not stable enough.

One of the residents shared her perceptions of the staffing changes during an informal conversation: 'In the beginning they were a lot more strict, they were more organized, and everything was clean – just so. Things were done at a certain time. The staff were older women. They knew more.'

The funding difficulties during the first couple of years also meant that Savard's was not self-supporting. The Homes First Society began to carry Savard's as a loss. There was talk in the air that Savard's could be, or should be, shut down. There were also discussions held by the Resource Group that the project should 'spin off' and become independent from Homes First. Residents asked me many times whether I knew if the project would be closing.

Savard's imperceptibly shifted away from operating as a staffing collective (in consultation with the advisory Resource Group), and in its second year the Homes First Society appointed an administrative manager. With management changes, and internal organizational changes, support for Savard's from the Homes First Society strengthened.

One of Savard's front-line staff declared, when the project had been open for almost three years, 'The Homes First Society has no desire to change it from what it originally started out to be, and does *not* want to shut it down. So I feel like *we've won*! And we're *not* moving away from the First Principles.'

Are we reaching the women we wanted to reach in the first place?

Under financial pressures from the outset, and with the necessity of being able to charge municipal Hostel Services per diems to keep the facility operating, Savard's opened its doors to some women who seemed more 'connected' to the 'system' than had originally been anticipated. For example, many were already receiving the Family Benefits Allowance. One of Savard's original staff mused during an interview: 'I guess the one surprise for me has been, some of the women that are with us. I had expected to be working with more people who very isolated, very uncommunicative, for whatever reasons. I was quite surprised to discover there were so many young women. This was news to me, that there were so many young women that couldn't stay housed because of mental health issues or behavioural problems. There was a little bit of learning for me there.' Another explained during an interview: 'I think they're out there. They're out there, the women who are more isolated. I think that there was a push. We were so under the gun for funding that there was a push to fill up. We knew that we couldn't wait too long. That it wasn't going to look too good if we only had four women, and that to reach women like Norma would take months and months and months of work on the part of HOP outreach. I think it might have been different had we secured two-year funding, and allowed to have that waiting period – where it was okay to just have three women in the house, or four women, or five women.' Street outreach with chronically homeless women can take months, if not years, before a woman may decide to come 'inside.'

During the time of my fieldwork, staff made arrangements for two women who came to live at Savard's to find accommodation elsewhere, after it became clear that they were 'higher functioning' (in the words of one staff member). They did not fit Savard's mandate to house long-term homeless women with severe mental health issues. This was difficult for some of the other women living at Savard's – they were worried that they too would be asked to move on.

Flexibility

The women living at Savard's make the space their own in terms of plotting their comings and goings any time of the day or night. Staff are available twenty-four hours a day to residents. The time 'envelope' could scarcely be more flexible.

The spatial 'envelope' is not as flexible. The sleeping modules constructed were far too massive and heavy for any one person to move, or even several to move. Instead of the nooks moving, the women moved. When a nook became available, it would perhaps be taken over by another resident. Others claimed one nook as their own.

With the requirement to house fifteen women rather than just ten, the nooks were shifted to make more room. During an interview three years after Savard's was opened, one of the administrators explained: 'Not necessarily everybody was happy with the changes. Some of the renovations and moving nooks around that we did at Savard's – there was a lot of resistance to. From both residents and staff. And in the end, people came back to say, 'It's working. It made sense to do that. Good move.' I think part of the reason is that people are still hooked on that ownership thing. And if you wanted to change, then it meant that we were doing something wrong. And you know change isn't about that. But sometimes, it ends up being translated that way. Or interpreted that way.'

At 2,000 square feet, however, Savard's is clearly too small a facility to accommodate fifteen women in residence, two staff, and visitors (for example, the public health nurse, a social worker, or ex-resident).

'When the house is really upset, people can't get out of each other's face. It's very small, very small, and very smoky,' one of the residents confided during an informal conversation.

While the sleeping nooks work well for some women, there is no room set off to allow a private conversation, for example, between a resident and staff. All takes place within the direct gaze and hearing of everyone else. The pacing and screaming room, once proposed, was dropped along the way under the pressure of square footage restrictions.

Concerns about fire were ongoing. Some of the women smoked in their nooks, despite staff 'policing.' One would throw her burning cigarette down on the floor after finishing it, as if she were still living out on the street. One day, a fire started in a garbage can and the can melted down. The fire alarm had malfunctioned and did not go off. Almost two years after the project opened, a fire inspector declared that the sprinkler system would not help if a fire did start. The ceilings of the nooks had to be removed.

Some of the women indicated wanting to have a private room. It is hoped that some day Savard's will have the opportunity to develop another site. (See the section entitled 'Post-Savard's' in Chapter 8.) This would allow women to move, should they so choose, from a relatively communal style of living to a mix of individual and shared spaces – yet still within a supportive environment. One of the staff interviewed three years after the project's opening, stated starkly: 'We're basically stuck in this space until we get a new one.' She quipped, 'They're not *nooks*. They're *crannies!*'

Involving the Women

During a staff meeting six months after the project opened, discussion centred on how the women could be directly consulted about the project's directions. One staff member commented at that meeting: 'There's never any sense of working with the women as a group. I don't think that's something that *can't* happen. I guess it would be wonderful if that did happen, but that's not my main objective. That's not what I see as part of it.' Another staff member then said: 'They're not clients because they aren't free to enter into a contractual relationship. They aren't patients, and they aren't residents [trailing off]. I guess residents is the proper term, but that sounds like an old folks' home to me. We always just say "the women," don't we?'

With the realization, as the months went by that many of 'the women' were indeed choosing to stay at Savard's, it became important to ask, should the women be consulted in more than informal or individual moments about their preferences? That key question was in fact posed by Resource Group members in the early planning discussions (and featured in Chapter 4): 'And at what point do women start to participate? What's the process of decision-making with residents? Many women with mental health problems are tremendously supportive and tolerant of each other' (Front-line worker, member of Resource Group, speaking during one of the planning meetings held in 1996.)

There was a clear shift from assuming that the women would not be interested in, or capable of having a say, in Savard's development. Interviewed when Savard's had been open for three years, one of Savard's staff (quoted at the beginning of this chapter) stated unequivocally: 'If we are client-driven, then there is a natural progression that happens with individual clients. So, if Ursula is going to be with us all her life, or at least for the next several years, what can we do to help her? So that her existence isn't about smoking all day, running to the corner store, to trade in those packs of cigarettes because Ursula has decided that she needs Vaseline. What else can we do? How do we work with Ursula to give her some sort of quality to her life? So that's she got some sort of dignity and respect. If we really say, we're client-driven, then I've got to involve her in the decisions that I'm going to make. And it can't be hands-off.'

Staff started to try weekly residents' meetings three years after the project opened – with tea and cookies around the dining room table. 'Please come and join us. Thought we could talk a while. What do you think?' The same staff member explained: 'The assumption was that women at Savard's couldn't do that, or we shouldn't ask them to do that, or that they wouldn't be interested in doing that, or wouldn't be capable of doing that. To me, it's okay if in the middle of a meeting one woman screams. Or another woman starts talking about something that has nothing to do with what we're talking about. But I think it means something if you can work with people to say, "What do you think, Ursula? Is the food okay? Do you feel like a different menu? Can we do something else? You guys interested in a field trip?" Ursula might go off and start talking about Harry and start talking about school and start talking about something else, but that's all right.' Reflecting more upon relations among residents, she used the metaphor of a 'blended family' to characterize budding dynamics:

I think the women at Savard's become family. With or without, or *in spite of* us. And I saw it in particular – we started moving new women in, and we had that core group there. It was almost as if it was sisters fighting with the step-sisters that were now part of the new family.

So, I just figure, if it's happening anyway, then let it happen with some sort of facilitation from staff. And then maybe we can control the bullying that might go on, and we can encourage ... use it to support. And you see that more and more with the women.

They'll actually go to bat whenever anyone has ever been taken from here to go to hospital or something. There's always at least half, if not three-quarters of the women that come right after she's gone to say, 'Is Martha coming back? Is it okay? Can I go see her in hospital? Can I?'

And that kind of stuff happens, I think, because relationships are formed, and partly it happens, I think, because it's a real fear to the women, when they see one woman getting taken out. Might that happen to *me*?

This staff member mused further about employment opportunities that some Savard's women were now able to take advantage of: 'All these things that you didn't think the women there could do – now, we pay the women inside the shelter to clean. And they love that! Because that gives them extra money in their pocket! They've done it in such a fair way. On their own, they came to staff and said, "We want to rotate the cleaning, so that all of us have a chance to make some money." So there's a little group of them, and that's what they do. One will do it for a week. Then the next one will do it for a week. It works out to about an hour a day.'

The Homes First Society set up a new job training department called 'Tenant's First' in 2000. This department was set up in response to shifting provincial funding mandates that required housing providers, such as the Homes First Society, to incorporate supportive programming for residents living in the projects they managed. Some of Savard's staff moved into this department, and at the time of the research, had facilitated three of Savard's residents to start job training.

Boundaries, Intervention, and Non-intervention

The keyword non-intervention is one that echoed through the planning, development and operation of Savard's. It is also a word that provoked the most questioning. One of the original staff interviewed said carefully:

> I think, in the beginning, I believed, that by letting women be, they would find what they needed to find. One, we didn't know the women. Two, we didn't know ourselves. Three, it was a way of building trust, by the non-intervention in the early stages. So I think empowerment, for them, initially was let them be. For once, they weren't being told that they had to do this, and they had to do that, and then they had to do this. In the first several months, we just let women be. You let them be and let them find their space and then you bring in the limits. We all need boundaries in our life ... I think we're not servicing one person, we're serving all the women. I need to deal with the mass, the crowd, and if one person's behaviour's affecting everybody, then it really is that one person that needs to go and take a walk.
>
> When they come in, we let them know, it's very informal in fact, that if they are screaming for long periods of time, it won't be tolerated if it affects the rest of the house. Violence won't be tolerated. Use of drugs in the house won't be tolerated. So there's that simple statement. But then you look at the complexity of what that statement means in the day-to-day running of things, and think of all the discussions built in – on and on and on – and so the statement is deceiving. Non-intervention – did it mean that we just did everything for them, and they did nothing?

Another of the original staff members also reflected during an interview: 'That balance between intervention and non-intervention, that balance, that changes every minute and every day.' She puzzled over what she termed the 'fuzzy boundaries' of stepping in, or not, and how these potentially related to staff's own biases:

> I haven't really thought it out, but the problems that bother the staff are the ones that get tended to the most. Like, for instance, cleaning up after Martha is a big problem. The smell of Martha is a *big problem*, so she became someone that they discussed and did something about.
>
> There's other women there that also have big problems, but maybe they don't impact on staff as much. Clara is one of them. I don't know what's happening with this woman. Nobody knows what's happening. She's been there for a year almost. It's hard to believe, and nothing's changed. She began to speak and she didn't speak before, but it's been a while since

she's been speaking. She listens to the radio, she does things like that. The first few months, I would say, yes she had to be left alone, and she really needed to. But I feel like some staff aren't approaching her because they don't know what's going to happen, because it looks like she could be quite violent.

But what about her? Her arms are a mess. Her hands are a mess. She smells terribly of dampness. Is that what we're supposed to be doing? Leaving her there, so that instead of her lying on the streets to sleep, she's at least got a warm bed to sleep in, and she's got food, and that's the end of it? I'm not clear that that's exactly where it's supposed to go ... I'm not too clear about that.

Maybe it's unfair to say this, but for instance, with Chris, they're doing something about Chris, because she could have assaulted the staff. Well, all the residents were in a lot of danger too, a long time before she threw a needle at anybody. I think sometimes things are dealt with because full-time staff get affected. Why are these decisions getting made? Based on us? How it's affecting us? How are these decisions made? When are they made? Why are they made? I don't think they're just completely non-interventionist reasons, because intervention does happen when it affects the staff!

During an informal conversation in Savard's staff office, one of the second-generation staff members declared, 'We've formed [had certified and committed for psychiatric assessment] four people in the last two months. You can't call that non-intervention. Of course, we're intervening!' The other staff member on shift that day laughed and said, 'We're intervening all the time!' Surreptitiously she opened the office door a crack, and stuck her head around the office door, and peered out into the house. She said in a hoarse whisper, 'This is intervention.' The two broke into gales of laughter, and continued to joke about non-intervention: 'Is this their home? Well, if this is their home, why do we tell them to leave? Why do we say, 'No, you can't have any more milk.' They don't have a key to the door. Is that a home?'

Another second-generation staff member was also very critical about what she termed the 'motto' of non-intervention. She pointed out that some women at Savard's did not respond at all well to the 'non-interventionist model.' In her mind, the key question could be put very succinctly: 'The discussion is, at what point do we intervene, instead of we're not going to intervene.' She described 'old staff versus new staff' tensions: 'Looking at Kay from January 1997 to now, Kay is perhaps in a worse situation because she eats and sleeps the whole day. She eats eggs every day. She doesn't do any form of exercise. She doesn't bathe. She doesn't brush her teeth for 365 days. When we talk about "intervention as non-intervention," we need to look at that and we need to look at the philosophy, and we need to look at the women we have at Savard's. What will happen to her? If she doesn't do certain things, you're intervening. The discussion is at what point do we intervene, instead of we're not going to intervene. We do intervene.'

She continued that some of the women had been asking for staff to arrange for activities. She felt frustrated and bound by Savard's avowed philosophy:

> Some of the residents have told me they'd like to have a meeting. But this is not our mandate, this is not our philosophy. The women have also requested us – can one of you take us to a swimming pool once a week? Or could we go to the Island? They do want us to intervene more. They do want us to do some kind of activity with them, and that has never been acknowledged. Because this is not what we do at Savard's. And I find that frustrating.
>
> There's no movement; there's no changes. It's just – you're providing housing to these women. That's all – it's only housing. There's not a model that empowers these women. There's not a skill – nothing! These women are not changing. They're just sitting there. We just give them a space to stay there. We're not a counsellor. We're a housing worker. We don't have to counsel these women. We don't have to do anything with them, and yet, we do cook for them. You sort of feel like your hand's been chopped. You can't do much. Because the mandate is non-intervention.
>
> Here we've got the de-institutionalization of the institution! That is just a concept. Intellectually, it's only a concept, because inevitably, you come to another form of institution, right?

She questioned Savard's mandate even more strongly:

> We do need to look at Savard's mandate, and certainly I see the many things wrong at Savard's that they need to be modified, they need to change. I really don't know what kind of changes yet, but this is one of them. You can't stand by, seeing a woman kill herself, when we can do some kind of work, use our skills, and do some kind of work with her. One of the women with diabetes used to drink seven bags of milk a day, and she was allowed to do that. That to me, you see, to me, was a ques-

tion, a moral question. I can't do this to a woman. She's going to die. So you offer her water, so I pulled the milk, until eventually we decide. Somehow we made the decision as a group to do that. But it takes a very long time to come to that decision – seven months! We can't treat Savard's as a house, and all these women as the same, because these women are not the same. They're different.

Another second-generation staff member reflected on what she termed 'intruding' on the residents:

You work with people, you ask them, 'What is it you'd like to see happen?' Some of the things we might be able to implement, some we might not. Why don't we just talk about it? And this *is* intrusive.

But is it not *intrusive* to do their laundry? Is it not intrusive to make dinner and we decide what we'd like to eat, not the women? I feel like I have tremendous power over these women. I do my service through my cleaning and my cooking, but I don't include the women in any decision-making. We buy plants. 'What plants would you like to see in this place?' 'Why don't we come up with a menu together?' This is the kind of thing I find really strange ... We're simultaneously being not intrusive, but we've been excluding the community we serve!

In what follows, several issues are explored that speak volumes about other tensions or clear shifts in Savard's daily practices. Highlighted are issues related to questions around non-intervention, small and large: 'Is there going to be a TV?' 'Will we be dispensing meds?' 'How will racist behaviours be dealt with?'

The Case of the TV

'Is there going to be a TV?' This question was asked at a 1996 Resource Group meeting. The decision was no. Concerns were that television was addictive, and those who had visited Women of Hope declared, 'They use TV to sedate their residents.'

During a staff meeting just after the project opened, staff also debated whether or not to have a TV at Savard's. The discussion was precipitated when one of the residents 'found' a TV and brought it into the house. Some staff argued for taking it out, but others countered:

'In theory, if we are allowing them to define their space [pause]?'

'The noise will disrupt people.'

'There will be lots of fighting over what to watch.'

'We're making an arbitrary decision. The space is getting smaller as we bring more and more women in.'

'I kind of like the silence.'

'I really don't like our deciding.'

'It's really arbitrary of us as a group – all-seeing, all-knowing.'

'I hate the idea of a TV.'

'Are we going to watch on a stolen TV?'

'It's very addictive.'

'I don't like the argument that *one* arbitrary decision may lead to other arbitrary decisions.'

[Silence.]

'If we can't reach consensus, shall we vote on it, or do we want to take it to the Resource Group?'

The TV discussion adjourned. A staff member interviewed one year after Savard's opened stated: 'The bottom line for me is that as much as we can, working with 10+ women, I still think we are as non-interventionist as can possibly be, and I really see that Savard's has worked so far. In a whole year we've only even had one discussion about permanently asking a woman to leave. She's still here, we have not asked any woman in the house to be medicated. And we don't have a TV that they sit in front of all day.'

One hot, hot summer day I was standing outside talking to one of the women about research. She turned to me, her eyes squinting against the sun, and said, 'You think I want anything to do with that other researcher from [a mental health treatment centre]? Why should I? Do you think I would trust them? They took my children from me. I was in there for two months. They were giving me drugs. I didn't want them to – don't trust any of them. Are we guinea pigs? Is this an experiment to see how people can live in an environment without television? If we had a television, there'd be a lot less fighting here. Are you watching us? How does that make you feel? You're studying us.'

I responded that it *was* awkward sometimes, and said to her, 'How do you share the lessons from here, to try and help others?'

'How do you think *we* feel?' she responded.

I said that the research I was doing was not to conduct an experiment about 'no TV.' I joked, 'I don't even have a TV myself.'

She greeted this with a hoot of laughter.

'I hope my research will be able to help other homeless women.' We went inside Savard's, and she offered me a glass of cold grape juice.

Many of the women at Savard's continued to express interest in having a television. Eventually, a TV did come to Savard's (and stayed) during its second year. Another resident brought it into the house. Staff revisited debates about whether to have a TV or not.

> 'We've come a long way without a TV.'
>
> 'We would try to go without it, but if people are storming the barricades [trailing off].'
>
> 'With the TV in the house, there've been a couple of fights over it. I had to unplug it.'
>
> 'Staff may have to bring in an authoritarian stance, which we don't want.'
>
> 'There's too much background noise in a small space. It may interfere when people are trying to sleep.'
>
> 'Residents are sleeping a lot earlier overall. It's such a different place than it was a year ago.'
>
> 'The women seem really bored.'
>
> 'We all have TVs at home!'
>
> 'What if we put the TV out at a specific hour?'
>
> 'That's very institutional. It's just as judgmental to say no TV – when most of western civilization has a TV.'
>
> 'We have talked to the women, and some want it. Others don't.'
>
> 'Have the women come up with their own rules on how to deal with conflict. Our concerns about addictions and exercise should remain with the staff team. Allow women to come to the decision themselves. See how they handle that. We can try it out.'

Dispensing Medication

In the beginning, Savard's staff would not dispense any medications for residents, nor would they keep medicines in the office. Savard's Relief Orientation materials (May 1997) stated categorically: 'Residents' medication is the responsibility of residents. Staff will *not* provide medication of any kind to residents, including over the counter cold and stomach remedies, aspirin, etc.' The intent was for women to take responsibility themselves for their own medications. One of the staff spoke about the tensions around medications on-site: 'I don't want the doctor coming in and pushing meds on people, and this is a real issue as far as I'm concerned. It's an issue to *not* have it happen, but it's also an issue, that if the client wants it, that it can happen. Particularly in women's theory and therapy and women's services, there's been a polarization. It's very confusing. There's a whole anti-medication [movement], but to not be able to say that there are some people who do and want to. They do function better on some medications, and want to take them. I'd hate to see them be propagandized into not taking them, if they felt they were helping them.'

Over time, it became apparent that not all the women who were taking medications were able to supervise their own medicines, and other residents were stealing some of the prescription drugs. Ten months after the project opened, staff were starting to hold medicines in the main office for some of the residents. One staff member expressed a sense of confusion and frustration:

> There's different treatment, and it can be perceived as unequal treatment. For instance, we don't hold L.'s medication. She's on Prozac, she's over-dosed, she's done it a few times. We don't hold M.'s medication either, yet we do it for B. And I think this is where it's very subtle, but it comes through in different treatment. So where is staff accountability now? This is a non-interventionist model. I find if x then y equals b or c, I begin to feel like I don't quite understand. What are the rules that are in place here? What's the logic here? The process has to be looked at again, and over and over again, if it's necessary. It should be something that's really joyfully done in order to try and learn. But I think it's very hard to revisit things over and over and over again.

Two years after the project's opening, one of the staff showed me the drawer of medications in the staff office. It was filled to the brim with bubble-pack bundles of tablets and pills. As she showed me the drawer, the staff member asked: 'How do you define non-intervention? Because if you're giving meds, that's intervening. What are our ethical obligations?' She lifted her shoulders and raised up her hands as the telephone rang, there was a knock at the door for delivery of groceries, one of the residents needed help with finding her address book, and another had just cut herself while she was working in the kitchen.

Racism

Savard's had been open for just over a year, when one evening, Teresa was on a rant. She harangued Donna for an hour. Several weeks later

Teresa also assaulted one of the staff members. After this, she was asked to leave for a period of two weeks. It was made clear to her that she could return to live at Savard's after this period, should she wish.

Teresa and Donna were both of mixed heritage. Donna told me that Teresa had called her 'nigger' and 'Aunt Jemima.' She continued, 'And staff did nothing. They say, she can't help herself, she can't help it. Now that's a judgement call. I told her you're black like me. But you know, she thinks she's white.' Donna confided, 'This place isn't safe. Why do I keep running? ... I've told staff I want to live here forever. This place isn't safe either. Some of the people who live here aren't very nice. Teresa, she's not a nice person. She hit one of the staff. Is that what you call safe? I'm asking you. And now she's going to be coming back here? Why are they letting her come back? Now that's not right. I left before because she was here. And notice she picked on the one staff who's not white? You see, I've got that all figured out. I put all these pieces together.'

Donna expected a system of reward and punishment. The ultimate punishment which shelters generally hold ransom over residents is barring or expulsion. At Savard's, there was no such ultimate punishment, even for verbal racist abuse. Where then is the line drawn between individual rights and collective security? At what point intervention? How to protect the vulnerable from the volatile?

One of the original staff I interviewed during this period was very concerned about the lack of clarity around this kind of racism. 'I don't think we do deal with it, and I think we have to deal with it. I think this is something we have to talk about more. And I don't think we've worked it out yet. I think we're a little immobilized still by our policy of non-intervention ... We're feeling immobilized.' In her words, 'We don't do anything. I have heard Teresa say some things that made me sick, physically feel sick, just awful stuff. Teresa seems to deny [her black heritage]. She does not acknowledge that in any of her self-talk. She completely externalizes. It's the other that's the person of colour. I find that really fascinating.'

Another second-generation staff member, herself black, read an article in which I had written about this incident (Bridgman 1999d). She critiqued the analysis with an acute awareness of power hierarchies. 'What is wrong if Teresa calls herself white? *Why is that a problem?* She's just as much white as she is black. It's this whole idea of a drop of blood contaminating white. And think of the power structures here. She's identifying with white. That's what's got the power here. That's a smart thing to do.'

During interviews, staff highlighted over and over the necessity for making daily decisions around intervention and non-intervention, particularly in relation to what one termed 'survivor culture': 'It's the whole thing around intervention, non-intervention, and when to intervene and when not to, and how much is the group dynamic versus the individual? When an individual is ranting, how much is it affecting the other people in the house?' She continued, 'We may think a woman's being affected, but they may not be. But my feeling is, well, they may act like they're not being affected, but I have to operate as if they are being affected, because they're tough. Their defences are so high. It's not in their culture to say, this hurts me, or this affects me, or this scares me, or this triggers something – that's not survivor culture, is it?'

Another second-generation staff member during an interview spoke about the danger of encouraging someone to leave the street – a primary intervention in and by itself – and then putting a time limit to that transition. She stated passionately:

We bring somebody in from the street, right? Women who meet our criteria. History of homelessness, severe mental health. So you work with people sometimes months, sometimes a year or more to get them indoors. You're going to do all that work to get them indoors, for what? For three months? So say, now your time is up – go back on the street so your space can be filled for another three months with someone else. That doesn't even make sense! At least, from my perspective, at least we're helping, on a long-term basis, thirteen or fourteen women, instead of on a very short-term basis.

Think about the whole criteria – the whole array of trying to reach women, the ones that are falling in the cracks, the ones that have been living on the street for years, it doesn't make sense that it could be only a temporary measure.

For another second-generation staff member, the unlimited period for staying at Savard's is an 'illusion':

I think it's a great view, but I see it as an illusion, because I think there's more than ten or fifteen women in the city. What happens to the other hundred women, two hundred women, in this city that desperately need [pause]? They all have a right to be at Savard's, and we can't, because we have these women forever in our place, right? The idea, I think, of having Savard's is wonderful, if we could only create 150 Savard's! The issue of homelessness, women who live with health issues, is huge. It's big! It's in our society. However, having a dozen women here doesn't resolve it at all, does it?

It's a total illusion to maintain something like this. And you know these women know. J. talks about, 'This is an illusion. I know this is. So, I have to enjoy this, because this is only going to be for a year or two, right?' They know places like that never exist.

Sanctions: Leaving, 'Zero Eviction,' and Being Asked to Leave

By the end of almost three years, five residents decided themselves to move on to self-contained apartments or into other housing options (for example, Strachan House). As stated earlier, arrangements were also made by staff for two women who did not fit Savard's target population to move to transitional housing.

Three former residents were back on the street, too fearful to stay, or they chose to return to the street, finding even Savard's relative flexibility too constrictive. They were maintaining regular contact with Savard's through telephone calls, dropping by (for a meal, to get warm, or to do laundry). They were welcome to stay, and the hope was that continued visits would help them make the transition from street to shelter.

Of the four who set up their own households, one returned to the street despite the supports that were in place to help her, and subsequently returned to Savard's to begin the process of recovery once again. Another lived at Savard's for almost two years, although she would regularly leave for two or three days at a time. She decided to depart Savard's for another transitional housing shelter. Subsequently, she decided she wanted to return to Savard's. She did come back, but ended up leaving once again. As related by one of Savard's staff during an interview:

> She did come back. When Frances came back in, and we first took her in, day-by-day, kind of on the emergency bed. She came in, she had about a thousand bucks. She gave staff the whole thing. You know Fran's always had money.
>
> Staff was holding the $1,000. She started the crack thing again. Kept coming back in the office, 'Give me some money. Give me some of my money.' Ended up leaving that night with Joanie. Went to a hotel, blew all their money on drugs and partying. And two days later came back and wanted to come back inside.
>
> And I said, 'No, Frances. We'll talk about it at staff meeting. You go to

another shelter for now. We'll help you get there and we'll talk about this. Because the way you came in, and the things you got involved with are not okay.' So we haven't heard from her again.

Another chose to leave on her own, also after having lived for a couple of years at Savard's. She had had a long history of drug use. The staff member related: 'She was timed out one night. She was stealing everything that wasn't nailed to the ground. She stole the petty cash box. She stole our VCR after we were so proud of having the VCR, for the women. And, she took everything. Everything that wasn't nailed down she took. She was stealing from residents. So she got timed out. Ended up at one of the Out of the Cold's. She moved out. Chose to move out. So that actually helped, because the women had the chance to again create a little bit of community among themselves. We told the supervisor there [at the Out of the Cold], that we would hold her bed. We would see what we could do. And in the end she chose to give it up.'

Chapter 4 highlighted a clear statement, or guiding ideal underlying the beginning ideas about Savard's. It was (and remains) an ideal that contrasts with the general practices of other shelters in Toronto. One of the Resource Group declared: 'Zero eviction – it's a basic principle that we accept homeless women as they are, without expecting change. *Without the expectations of change.*'

During the time of the research, one woman was barred after she started sexually assaulting one of the other women. This was after many months of attempting to accommodate her, arranging her admittance for psychiatric treatment, and her subsequent return. In this case, the needs of the many prevailed over the needs of the one.

Savard's continues to be distinct in its relatively fluid rules about who can stay, who cannot, and for how long. Sanctions are administered at the discretion of staff on shift. A resident can be asked to leave for a period of hours, or for a twenty-four-hour period, for verbal abuse or particularly disruptive behaviour. A resident can also be asked to leave for a longer period of time. (Staff arrange for a bed at another facility, and provide for transportation.) In either case, the 'critical incident' is logged in the critical incident book. The circumstances are carefully reviewed at shift change, and then at the next staff meeting.

Conclusion

Staff working at Savard's three years after it opened had very different ideas about the meaning of intervention than some in the original staffing group had. These differences are neatly encapsulated by one second-generation staff member's pithy remark: 'That was then, and this is now.' For some, it was clear the whole idea of non-intervention was a fallacy and an absurdity. For one staff member, it was imperative to recognize that intervention, and the presence of staff, had to be acknowledged, and just as carefully and thoughtfully weighed. The Savard's model involves self-reflexivity about 'soft interventions,' a phrase used by Sylvia Novac, Joyce Brown and Gloria Gallant in their 1999 report entitled, *Women on the Rough Edge*.

According to one staff member I interviewed three years after Savard's opened: 'Maybe a lesson is, being non-interventionist is not useful. Which is great, because then that's a lesson. Or that it's useful for some women, and the longer those women stay in a place – where it's non-interventionist – the more they crave intervention. Work with them, see what happens.' Another staff member interviewed declared, 'If the women there do not feel that the staff are in control of what's happening, people start getting triggered. Because they become afraid that the bully there is going to run the show, and staff isn't going to stop her. As soon as there is a staff that the women know has things under control, and will not let violence happen, will not let unfairness happen, everybody just calms right down. So to me, the whole idea of intervention is up! You can't observe when you, as an observer, impact on the result. So that whole idea of objectivity and so – how can we be there and not intervene when our presence there impacts on what's happening? There's no such thing as me sitting in the office and they don't see me there. *Let's acknowledge that.*'

During one of the vision day sessions held in 1999, almost two and a half years after the project opened, staff had acknowledged that non-intervention was a term that everyone was familiar with, but it 'manifested itself as more of an immobilizing force rather than a progressive model of service delivery.' After reviewing what staff were actually doing in their work, and what they *would* like to be doing, they identified the following: 'We work with women where they are at. There is no compulsory program nor are there conditions for staying. Identify one or two staff as primary workers for each woman to help with consistent and clear communication. Work with women within individualized time frames, from a "let them be" approach (characterized as phase 1) through to when women can begin to identify goals (characterized as phase 2). Review possibility of house meetings, or small gatherings of women. Involve "women's voices." Review women's

abilities to contribute towards the house (for example, through minimal chores). Women approach staff with their own needs.'

Through all the discussions, the group kept referring back to the original principles to check themselves. Consensus grew that there had been
shifts in the operation of Savard's. They linked these shifts with the
newness of the pilot project (an experiment); funding instability; pressure to fill all the beds almost immediately; theoretical expectations
about the women's behaviour in contrast to experiences in daily
practice; staff–management conflicts and organizational restructuring;
interpersonal and generational conflicts among Savard's staff members; lack of a clearly defined relationship between the Homes First
organization, Savard's staff, and the Advisory Resource Group; and an
unclear understanding of Savard's underlying philosophy given staffing changes. Amidst all these issues, the voices of the women, the residents, had been lost.

The staffing group renewed the commitment to learning from the
'strengths, skills and survival abilities of the women' and '[determining]
what, if any, supports, programs and services they want.' In preparation
for the 1999 visioning day, staff were able to consult with seven of the
women to solicit their opinions about Savard's and its current practices.
They developed a basic questionnaire, which included some of the following questions. I have summarized the results briefly as follows:

How long have you been at Savard's? 2½ months to 2 years
What do you like about Savard's? 'Staff.' 'The area is not too high class.'
   'In-and-out freedom.' 'Vacation for two weeks [referring to having a
   bed held for two weeks after last contact].' 'Don't have to go out.'
   'Support, meals, safe environment.'
What do you not like? 'It's unhealthy [the odour].' 'Disorderly conduct of
   other residents.' 'Area is plain. I don't know if they're tearing things
   down or building them up [referring to construction in the gentrify-
   ing King Street–Dufferin Street area].'
Do you like your nook? 'It's practical.' Three replied yes. One explained
   the nook was too cold. 'Good for people with little or no money.'
   'Comfortable – don't change anything.'
Would you like a private room or a shared room? Two replied no. Three
   replied yes. 'Like the cooperative setting.' 'Would like shared room.'
Do you like it when staff intervenes in conflicts? One replied, 'It's not my
   business.' Four replied yes. One replied, 'When and if it's necessary.'
   'I like it when it's quiet.' 'Staff is fair.'

Do you like it when staff let women sort out their own conflicts? Two replied yes. One replied that staff is inconsistent. One replied, 'Depends on the conflict.' 'I don't know.'

Do you like it when staff give you your medication? Three replied yes. One said no. One said it's not applicable. One said, 'Either way is okay.'

Do you think we need more rules? An overwhelming 'No!' One said, 'Just enforce the ones we have.'

Other questions included: Would you like activities during the day? Would you go elsewhere for day activities? What are your long-term goals? Is Savard's helping you reach those goals? And what can we do to help reach them?

Asking residents very directly for their feedback was never proposed during the early years of the project. Yet the staffing group working at Savard's at this point felt it important to involve residents in decisions about running Savard's.

Expectations around behaviour at Savard's are still nominal. Staff impose time-out periods (from two hours to several days) for violations of Savard's few rules around no substance use on-site, no weapons, and no violence (for example, physical violence or verbal racist insults). Arranging for a resident to be admitted for psychiatric assessment is done only as a last resort (and after many attempts to consult with the resident). This action is reserved for instances when a woman is threatening other residents or staff in an ongoing targeted way, or is self-harming.

Some residents have stabilized and decided to move to other living arrangements. Several women who have left Savard's to return to the streets continue to maintain contact and return for companionship and a meal, to do laundry, and even to sleep the night. Some residents clearly wish to remain living at Savard's and have made gains in their health. Other residents have themselves asked for a somewhat more structured environment.

Community development – never a phrase used during any of the planning meetings of the Resource Group, nor during Savard's first couple years of operation – is a concept that has begun to feature in staff's perceptions about the dynamics at Savard's. Interestingly, the concept had been highlighted by one of the city's housing officials (Yamashita 1995) as the model to which the City of Toronto should aspire in its programs to alleviate homelessness. (See the discussion about Toronto's community development continuum as distinct from the U.S. continuum of care approach in Chapter 4.)

This chapter has explored some of the shifts in Savard's operation during a three-year period. Guylaine Racine suggests that the development of services for the homeless are not simply linked to the 'instinct for survival' of the organization nor to an a priori definition of the problem (1993:251–2). Rather, as with the case of Savard's, a number of factors affect the design of a project including the political, economic, and policy contexts in which the service arises, the perspectives of the actors engaged in developing the service, the specific group that has difficulty accessing services, and the fact those using the services can equally well transform that service.

CHAPTER EIGHT

Long Road from the Street

Many of the women who live at Savard's have had intermittent contact with Toronto's shelter system, but 'chose' to live on the streets. Some are barred from other shelters, or placed on contracts that limit their hours of stay, because of their aggressive or 'irrational,' even bizarre behaviours. They are also excluded from existing supportive housing for the same reasons that they are not welcome in the hostels. Following are three profiles of women who came to live at Savard's during the time of my fieldwork. These women were struggling to survive on the streets with limited, if any, options prior to living at Savard's. The profiles are drawn from a November 1998 program description written by staff of the Homes First Society. I have edited them for confidentiality and clarity.

Susan

The Hostel Outreach Program (HOP) received a call from a supportive housing agency that was in the process of evicting Susan for non-payment of rent. Agency staff were quite concerned about her physical and mental health but also felt unequipped to deal with her any longer. She was refusing to go to a shelter and had already been seen outside in cold weather wearing only a summer dress. It appeared that Susan would end up on the street. HOP asked a local doctor (who had seen Susan as a patient on previous occasions) to see her before she was evicted. The doctor decided that Susan needed to be hospitalized for both mental and physical health concerns. She was admitted to a hospital for a brief stay. HOP also talked with her about Savard's. Susan agreed to go – as long as people would not ask her questions upon her arrival. She did not want to stay at the hospital and left before many of her physical health concerns were resolved. While she was living at Savard's, it was discovered that Susan had a debilitating illness. Treatment for this started. Susan also received information and education about her illness.

Nettie

Nettie had been known to HOP for at least ten years and had ongoing contact with the program. Nettie had a lengthy history of living in hostels and was on most barred lists for aggressive and disturbing behaviour. She spent time in jail and psychiatric institutions. Occasionally, she would get her own room in the private market, but generally ended up being evicted after not paying rent or having difficulties with other tenants. Nettie became lost to HOP after moving in with friends in 1995. She resurfaced again in late 1996, in the worst condition, both mentally and physically, that staff could remember. She said she had been in jail and had been living on the street since her release. HOP initiated a referral to Savard's. Nettie moved in, and after living there for a couple of years, became remarkably well, and was interested in seeking her own apartment.

Phoebe

Phoebe came to the attention of HOP through calls from both the police and social workers at a downtown emergency department during the winter of 1997. Phoebe had been on the streets for approximately nine months. She generally refused to go to hostels. When she was taken there on occasion by the police (who became concerned for her well-being), she would only stay a few hours or would be asked to leave (for example, for smoking in non-designated smoking areas and asking other residents repeatedly for cigarettes). She had come to Toronto from an outlying area, after being asked to leave a group home. Prior to living in this group home, she had spent most of her adult life hospitalized for her mental health problems.

When the street outreach workers caught up with her, Phoebe was not dressed at all appropriately for the winter weather. She did not seem to be aware of this and showed no interest in her own well-being. The street outreach team facilitated an admission for Phoebe to a downtown hospital, where she became somewhat stabilized. She did not want to go to a group home or boarding home again. She also refused to go anywhere she thought she might be asked to leave or that would ask her many questions. The HOP team agreed that she would not survive the intake procedures for mainstream supportive housing. They told Phoebe about Savard's. They assured her Savard's staff would not ask a lot of questions. She was interested in visiting Savard's. Once there, Phoebe agreed to stay. She maintained connections with her HOP worker and had psychiatric follow-up as well. It was her doctor's opinion that, without Savard's, Phoebe would most likely be hospitalized on a long-term basis.

Savard's has been able to help women such as Susan, Nettie, and Phoebe stabilize their lives. What lessons does the Savard's model suggest? This chapter offers concrete insights about what kinds of interventions work and outlines some of the conditions that can hinder or facilitate such interventions. Lessons relate to philosophy, funding, design, administration and staffing, outreach and referrals, intake, support services, evaluation, and post-Savard's.

Philosophy

Savard's low-demand, high-support mandate requires staff be available twenty-four hours a day, seven days a week to provide flexible, individualized support. If need be, they can quickly intervene in situations that, in other facilities, would probably result in a woman being asked to leave. There is a high staff-to-client ratio, and staff are readily able to get to know the women on their own terms and to provide supportive counselling. They can also help the women begin to link with other resources.

The model offered by Savard's rests upon a tolerant and non-judgmental foundation, with few rules, no expectations to attend house meetings, and a general policy of not requiring goal-oriented contractual forms. Nor are women expected to attend day programs. Residents are encouraged by staff to keep doctors' appointments, to take medication if this has been prescribed for them, and to attend to their personal care and hygiene, but the responsibility for these activities rests with the women themselves. Psychiatric treatment for women is not a required part of the model, but it may be sought in instances where a woman's behaviour has become a serious threat to her own safety or the safety of others.

One staff member, when asked about her job duties, emphasized the importance of 'interacting with the women on their terms':

> We clean a lot of toilets [laughter], cook a lot of meals. And I interact with the women on their terms basically. If you see somebody is in a delusional state of mind, for example, saying that she was born, she lives in England. And then she was born again on the boat going over to Canada. And then she lived in Sri Lanka and she was born again. She's been born lots and lots of times, then you know what? I stick with that. If that's where she's at, in what she believes, then I stick with it. I'd go with the delusional. I think being willing to work with women on their terms is very, very important – being able to inject some humour into the day too. I would say that's part of the job description. And then, of course, hooking up with other services if women want that, the paper work, and the food ordering, and all the stuff that has to get done.

The length of time that a woman stays at Savard's is highly individualized. Visitors are not allowed inside Savard's in keeping with its safe haven mandate (see section entitled 'Post-Savard's,' about accommodation of ex-residents). It is expected that many of the women will want to move on to more independent forms of housing, after a period of stabilization in a high-support environment. Some women take a long time to move; others want to stay. Both groups are accommodated, as there is no restriction on length of stay.

The research highlights the difficulty of planning to accommodate the needs of a segment of society's most marginalized groups – chronically homeless mentally ill women. It also highlights a dialectic in planning such programs. By their very nature, administrative frameworks tend to impose structure that may conflict with the needs of individuals that require flexibility. How can this contradiction be successfully reconciled? The simple, yet complex, answer is that there will always be trade-offs. The kind of shelter model offered by Savard's can only accommodate a very small number of women.

Given the identified risks of abuse and violence for many homeless women (first as children, and then at the hands of male partners), it is important for women-only emergency facilities and housing options (such as Savard's) to be available.

Funding

It would seem obvious that the survival of a demonstration project, no matter how visionary, can be threatened without stable funding in place. It has been incumbent upon the Homes First Society to demonstrate and defend, over and over again to funders, what is unique about the project's approach. If Savard's is to be defined as providing transitional housing, who defines how long those transitions may take? Government policy advisers? Front-line staff? Administrators? Homeless women themselves? Savard's working philosophy clearly privileges the power of chronically homeless women themselves to determine the pace. Yet, their rhythms do not necessarily keep pace with staff's perceptions, nor with the mandates set by government funding agencies. Without the security of long-term funding, staff morale can be jeopardized, and fragmentation of efforts and loss of resolve can ensue.

Design

At 2,000 square feet (the square footage of many single family dwellings!), Savard's is too small for fifteen residents and two staff. The (generally acknowledged as private) functions of the residents dressing, conversing on the phone with a brother or sister, consulting the visiting nurse, all take place within a highly circumscribed small world a scant twenty feet from the sidewalk.

Savard's could easily do with twice the space. There is currently no private meeting space for visiting health care workers, for example, nor for staff to meet with residents individually. The storage area is small. The staff room is extremely small, particularly during shift change, when up to four staff consult on issues arising that need immediate follow-up. The staff room should also have been designed originally with two means of access. This became apparent during one critical incident when staff was assaulted by a resident. The other staff member was unable to exit from the staff room, with another resident blocking the way. Future facilities are discussed in the section entitled 'Post-Savard's.' (See also the Epilogue.)

Administration and Staffing

One important issue in Savard's operation has been to ensure that communication channels for full-time staff and relief staff remain consistent and strong. Relief staff work at many different projects managed by the Homes First Society. Savard's operating philosophy is unique among Homes First projects, and relief staff have not always understood Savard's working philosophy. In turn, administrators and full-time staff have not always been able to include relief staff in their decision-making and consultation processes. One of the Savard's relief staff interviewed spoke about feeling excluded during the early years of Savard's: 'A number of us felt that we had come to Savard's with lots of skills from other jobs. It wasn't the first women's shelter I'd ever worked at, and with some of the other relief staff, we didn't really feel that we were included as part of the team there. We weren't invited to meetings at all.'

These issues were linked to larger organizational and union issues within the Homes First Society. Along the same vein, Savard's was first developed by a group quite independent of the Homes First Society. During its early stages of operation, there were tensions between the vision developed by the initial Resource Group and the general operating procedures of Homes First. With the departure of the original staffing group, and shifts in Homes First management, these tensions began to be resolved.

Clear channels of communication are required for all those involved in developing a project such as Savard's. The importance of this can be seen from the following declaration by one of Savard's staff during a time when many new staff were coming on board:

> It is a stressful job. You're on site for twelve and a half hours, you're there two days and one night, or one day and two nights. You have no break for lunch, you have no break for coffee, you have no break for tea, you work with the same person – 2-1-2, two shifts with one person and one shift with another.
>
> If you don't get on well with that person, think how hard it's going to be! If you have to also train your two co-workers, it could take up to four months. People don't always have the same philosophy. So, it's not like you're speaking to the converted, 'cause you have to do that philosophical stuff, as well as just the day-to-day stuff.

Staff require time to develop a common and consistent working philosophy and a sense of the 'team,' and to reflect on the evolution of the project. Working with chronically homeless women is difficult work, with a high turn-over rate and the danger of burn-out for many workers. Without clear attention given to team-building, there can be a lack of cohesiveness among the staff. The potential for conflict is rife, especially when people work twelve-hour shifts, and have several days off between their shifts. One staff member was articulate: 'We work on our own preconceived ideas, no matter how open you go in. It's a case of people with all good intentions going in different directions.'

One staff member explained: 'The intimacy of the job means that you know when the women get up. We know what they're eating. They know when we use the bathroom. We're all getting our periods at the same time – that classic group of women together, cyclically having their menstruation together. We're pretty much all on the same cycle within seven days.' Such intimacy requires care on the part of staff to be very clear about boundaries. The staff member explained further: 'We had a problem with one woman who was desperately ill, who was incontinent because of her coughing. And we were having to help undress her ... and now her throwing back in our faces that we like to look at naked women!'

Orientation sessions and 'vision days' help staff to evaluate their work in an ongoing fashion. Program areas or operating procedures may need to be developed in response to current needs – or staff may need to remember ideals that have been neglected.

Outreach and Referrals

The Hostel Outreach Program (HOP) makes the majority of the referrals directly from its street outreach program and also coordinates referrals from other agencies. Two of the beds are presently tagged as emergency beds, to be filled by full-time staff, on an as-need basis, as long the women meet the criteria of mental health issues and homelessness. Ex-residents also know about these drop-in beds and use them, and referrals come from other shelters in the city – shelters that also work with homeless mentally ill women, but operate with limits on how long the women can stay.

Criteria for encouraging a woman to live at Savard's are that the woman is living on the street and/or is having unsuccessful contact with the hostels. She is also experiencing mental health difficulties. It is important that the women coming into Savard's have developed trust with at least one person through HOP and from that trust are often willing to consider Savard's. The outreach process can be a long one, with many months between the time of first broaching the idea of Savard's and a woman actually coming to live there. HOP outreach workers continue to provide support once a woman has moved into Savard's – this provides continuity for the women.

Intake

The intake process is informal and non-intrusive. HOP staff generally discuss all potential referrals with the staff of Savard's, and then a time is set up for the woman to visit. When a person comes to Savard's for a visit or to stay, there is no formal intake interview. No application forms are filled out or signed. There is no search of personal belongings. These issues were all identified very early in the planning stages as barriers for some homeless women to access housing. This seems to be an important part of making the transition from street to shelter. Residents are not required to sign shelter forms either, once they live at Savard's. There is also a standing policy that a woman's bed and nook are hers as long as contact has been kept. Only when a woman leaves Savard's, and has not been in contact for two weeks, will her place be opened to others. Contact may take even the minimal form of a phone call or dropping in for a few hours. Should a woman be hospitalized or in jail, but it is expected that she will be returning to Savard's, her place will also be kept.

Support Services

A temporary Health Component Working Group was set up in 1996 before the project opened to serve as a resource for Savard's. Partnerships with local medical facilities were put in place, including dental staff, nutritionist, foot specialist, general practitioner, psychiatric services, public health personnel, and a local hospital. One of the important issues was to find supportive partners who would complement Savard's working philosophy. While some social service providers and health care professionals do visit residents at Savard's, there was a clear decision from the beginning that these services would not be mandatory for residents. In other words, their access to housing was not to depend on their willingness to engage with such professionals. As one health care professional from the local mental health centre put it, 'You're not expected to provide the kinds of things that a health care institution would have to provide. You're coming at this from housing.' Community agencies off-site have also offered supportive services for Savard's residents.

The Resource Group (front-line workers from women's shelters and drop-ins from across the city) instrumental in envisioning, planning, problem-solving, and implementing Savard's continued to meet for approximately a year after the project opened. The function of the group shifted from being a primary development force to becoming an advisory group. This transition happened as the Homes First Society took ownership of the project. Once the project opened, the working relationship between the original Resource Group and Homes First Society (administrators and Savard's staffing group) was not without tensions concerning the founding principles underlying the project and what form non-intervention should take.

Post-Savard's

Several ex-residents visit Savard's and telephone on a regular basis. They enjoy the occasional meal there, as well as a sense of community and support from staff. Some stay overnight occasionally to sleep in one of the emergency beds or on one of the sofas. It is felt by staff that this support is important for helping women maintain their housing, by reducing their sense of isolation.

At the time that Savard's was being developed, there was little discussion about how women could move on from Savard's. With active linkages between Savard's and its neighbour, Strachan House, being forged over time, several women have moved from Savard's into Strachan House. These ex-residents are easily able to return to Savard's for companionship and support.

During the fieldwork, discussions were under way about the possibility of finding a larger site and developing a graduated supportive congregate housing project. This would allow Savard's residents to move, should they choose, from a relatively communal open-concept style of living to a mix of privatized individual spaces and shared facilities – yet still within a high-support, low-demand environment designed for women. Savard's provides a transitional service for some chronically homeless women, but this depends on the availability of next-stage supportive housing for the women. (See the Epilogue.)

Evaluating Success

At the end of two and half years, five residents had been able to move on to self-contained apartments or into other housing options (for example, Strachan House). Three former residents were back on the street. They were too fearful to stay or chose to return to the street, finding even Savard's relative flexibility too constricting. They were maintaining occasional contact with Savard's through phone calls or dropping by for a meal. Of four who had set up their own households, one returned to the street despite the supports that were in place to help her. She subsequently returned to Savard's to begin the process of recovery once again. A fifth left Savard's to live in another of the city's transitional shelters.

Assessing the 'success' of Savard's has relied on very modest indicators in some cases. It is often difficult to observe any obvious improvements in women's lives beyond their very ability to stay at Savard's. This is important to keep in mind when assessing the worth of the project.

Another indicator centres on the predilection of the women for sleeping during the day, and staying up at night (an adaptive survival strategy for avoiding assaults). This pattern gradually shifted (over the first year of the project) to more women being wakeful during the day. Some women have been able to stabilize more quickly than others, and to move on. Others require a much longer period of time to stabilize. So-called gains or changes for them are imperceptible.

It is crucial that markers of success and indicators of progress for any program be generated at 'street level' in order to appreciate the subtleties of change that chronically homeless women may be able to make in their transitions from street life. As Paola Grenier acknowledges, prolonged homelessness requires certain adaptations for survival (such adaptations generally occur in as little as three weeks), and these make it increasingly difficult for people to return to the rhythms of mainstream society (Grenier 1996, cited in Novac, Brown, and Gallant 1999).

In work with chronically homeless women, close attention must be paid to the kinds of data by which the 'success' of a project may be judged, and therefore funded. Participant observation yields multiple insights about such success through spatial analysis, tracking patterns of use over an extended period, and qualitative interpretive analysis of the 'unspoken' (non-verbal) as well as the 'spoken.'

It is important to emphasize the value of extended ethnographic research to document the development processes for a project such as Savard's. The slow incremental changes and decisions that homeless mentally ill women make can only be appreciated over time. To suggest that such changes may take place overnight denies the reality of many of these women's lives.

The support and provision of basic needs offered by Savard's decreases the need for expensive in-patient admissions to emergency, acute or chronic care, or for prison institutions quite unequipped to help with the complex issues faced by long-term homeless mentally ill women. At Savard's, fifteen women are housed for approximately $600,000 annually. The cost for providing adequate acute psychiatric care for these women ($360 per day) would amount to almost $2,000,000 annually. Prisons and detention centres ($124 per day) would be approximately $700,000 for a year, according to a report prepared for the City of Toronto Mayor's Homelessness Action Task Force (Pomeroy and Dunning 1998:22).[1] These figures do not consider quality-of-life issues.

Provincial legislation, such as the Ontario Safe Streets Act (in effect 1 February 2000) to 'clean up' homeless people from the streets, and to prohibit vagrancy offences such as begging and the subsistence activities of squeegeeing youth, portends increasing policing of the homeless and the criminalization of homelessness. As well, Bill 68 (in effect 1 December 2000), a mental health reform package of amendments to the Canadian Mental Health Act and Health Care Consent Act, approves involuntary committal and enforced treatment for those deemed suffering from mental illnesses. Within these contexts, Savard's working philosophy stands in stark contrast indeed.

Savard's helps to repair the rents in the lives of chronically homeless women: lives that in many cases have been crossed with abuse, whether emotional, physical, or sexual, and unstable housing even as children – productive lives disrupted by mental illness. To end with the words of one Savard's staff member:

> She's somebody's daughter.
> She's somebody's mother.
> She is a woman who lives the life of a woman who has been abused.
> I think she is a survivor of childhood sexual abuse.
> I think she is a survivor of abuse in her family.
> I think she is a survivor.
> She ultimately,
> bottom line is,
> who has the right to say, she's not worth it?
> She's a survivor, she's a human being

and she's in a great deal of pain ...
These may not be the best days of her life ...
She's one of us, you know.
She is a mother.
She is a daughter.
She's a sister.
If you have any compassion for the hurt,
then she deserves what we can give her.

EPILOGUE

Savard's closed its doors 8 October 2002 ...
but re-opened them the same day in a new site.

The fifteen women then living at Savard's moved to the new place, and after one week, several others moved in a few at a time. In contrast to the old Savard's, the new Savard's now accommodates thirty women with twenty-two dorm-style single beds and two semi-private rooms (two beds each) on the second and third floors of a three-storey store-front. The administrative office, kitchen, and dining area are on the ground floor, with lounging sofas and chairs on the basement level. The team of front-line workers has expanded to include a life skills counsellor, housing outreach worker, and a cook/meal program educator, as well as a part-time cleaner.

The site of the old Savard's was converted into next-stage housing for Savard's residents, and became part of Strachan House. Its first residents were the last five women to be moved from StreetCity before it finally closed its doors in May 2003.

Support, assistance with housing readiness, life skills, and advocacy have become a more prominent part of Savard's profile, but there are still no time limits on how long a woman may live at Savard's, nor is there a front-door curfew – although the dorm floors are to be quiet after midnight. A non-smoking policy has been imposed, given concerns about fire safety issues, and Savard's now receives its funding directly from the Ministry of Health.

Notes

Chapter 1: Introduction

1 Articles arising from this research have explored design issues in developing housing for chronically homeless people (Bridgman 1999e), the street as a metaphor in the lives of the homeless (Anderson 1997; Bridgman 1999b), the idea of a 'city within a city' for street people (Bridgman 1998a), and the role of public art in housing for the homeless (Bridgman 1999c). A book manuscript, *StreetCities: Housing the Homeless in Toronto*, is in preparation. For a project description of StreetCity (written by the Homes First Society), see the report, 'Documentation of Best Practices Addressing Homelessness' (Canada Mortgage and Housing Corporation 1999b:69–94).

2 The Homes First Society was incorporated as a charitable organization in 1983. Their mission is to ensure affordable and permanent housing for people who are homeless and have the fewest options in Canadian society. At the time of my fieldwork, Homes First had developed and was managing 17 housing projects, including several targeting single mothers, women escaping violence, refugees, low-income families with children, and psychiatric survivors. They had approximately 850 tenants.

3 Some parts of this chronicle of Savard's history draw upon previously presented or published materials and expand upon their insights (Bridgman 2002b, 2001a, and 1999d).

4 Strachan House (with Savard's) represents one of the last social housing projects built with provincial funding, before the then newly elected Conservative government in Ontario announced massive cutbacks in June 1995 to social housing programs. There was a moratorium on all new projects, and funds already committed were clawed back. A total of 385 housing projects, totaling 16,732 units of housing operating by non-profit agencies throughout the province were cancelled. In the City of Toronto, 22 out of

32 projects were cancelled. Only those projects too far along in construction to be cancelled without serious litigation proceeded. Strachan House was the last project for which the Homes First Society received funding. The $4,000,000 budget for the whole project was secure only because the dollars had already been issued directly from the provincial Treasury Board, and not from the Ministry of Housing.

5 The words *hostel* and *shelter* are often employed interchangeably in Canadian usage, although hostels can refer to youth hostels for travellers. The word *hostel* is also associated with lodging that provides a bed and one or two meals. *Shelters* tend to be associated with accommodation and supportive social services.

6 Homeless women with children are relatively new to the growing homeless population, and they represent a group with needs distinct from homeless women with no children, and homeless women without their children present (Smith and North 1994: 602). The number of families admitted to hostels in Toronto increased by 76% from 1988 to 1996. In 1996, hostel admissions to children included 5,300 children (Springer, Mars, and Dennison 1998; Mayor's Homelessness Action Task Force 1999: 50).

7 There were a few discussions about my collaborating with the Queen Street Mental Health Center researchers. Their 'environmental scan' research was part of a community partnership arrangement between the Homes First Society and the center. Their study took place over an 18-month period, from January 1997 (when Savard's opened) to June 1998. My independent research had already begun two years earlier. My research was also continuing beyond the bounds of their study, and so this research collaboration did not happen. Our two studies were quite separate. A brief case study description (two pages) of Savard's was also written by several of those involved in developing Savard's. This write-up was included in the report 'Women on the Rough Edge: A Decade of Change for Long-Term Homeless Women' (Novac, Brown, and Gallant 1999:17-19).

8 *Utopia: The Search for the Ideal Society in the Western World* (Schaer, Claeys, and Sargent 2000) was published on the occasion of an exhibition organized jointly by the New York Public Library and the Bibliothèque nationale de France. This book provides readers with a fascinating review of the history of utopia – a rich visual and textual feast.

9 Jo Anne Schneider (2001) provides a good overview of ethnographies on organizations and ethnographic contributions to public policy formation (particularly social welfare reform), program implementation, and research on organizations and program participants.

10 I have published the stories of several homeless Aboriginal women whom I met in the course of my research at StreetCity and Strachan House (Bridgman 2000, 2001b). Drawing on the work of Lionnet (1995), these articles asked: 'How does she name herself in her own narratives? How does she find meaning in her own experiences?'

Chapter 3: Shelter Women

1 Evans and Wekerle (1997) also highlight women's vulnerability in the Canadian housing market.
2 There has been a spate of reports on homelessness and housing in Toronto (many commissioned by the Mayor's Homelessness Action Task Force for its 1999 report). Since 1996, included among the reports are *Back to Community: An Assessment of Supportive Housing in Toronto* (Novac and Quance 1998); *Better Access, Better Care* (Kushner 1998) *Borderlands of Homelessness: Women's Views on Alternative Housing* (Novac, Brown, Guyton, and Quance 1996); *Homeless Voices: Follow-up to Homeless, Not Helpless* (Ward and Tremblay 1998); *Mental Illness and Pathways into Homelessness* (Mental Health Policy Research Group 1998); *Locally Based Approaches to Prevention and Rescue from Homelessness* (Ward 1998a); *A Planning Framework for Addressing Aboriginal Homelessness in the City of Toronto* (Obonsawin-Irwin Consulting 1998); *The Role and Function of Emergency Hostels in Dealing with Homelessness* (Ward 1998b); *Report of the Provincial Task Force on Homelessness* (Ontario Provincial Task Force on Homelessness 1998); and *Taking Responsibility for Homelessness: An Action Plan for Toronto* (Golden et al. 1999).
3 Jennifer Wolch and Michael Dear (1993) in their book, *Malign Neglect*, link global economic and political forces to the experiences of individuals and communities in Los Angeles. Economic restructuring, erosion of affordable housing, divergent geographies of jobs and housing, and dismantling of the welfare state all conspire to push individuals to homelessness.
4 Other studies in which Sylvia Novac was involved have also highlighted the fact that many women would prefer to live in sex-segregated buildings (Novac, Brown, and Gallant 1998; Novac, Brown, Guyton, and Quance 1996; Quance and Novac 1996).
5 In Chapter 2 of her book *Homelessness in Global Perspective*, Irene Glasser offers a solid overview of the issues that homeless men have faced historically and the range of services available to them. She observes: 'Homeless men, historically the largest group of homeless people, receive only the most meager responses to their problems. Their independence and the pub-

lic perception of them as threatening, as alcoholics, and as mentally ill put this group last on the list for help' (1994:37). Gerald Daly (1996:132–5) also offers an excellent summary of the contrasting reasons for men and women to become homeless, together with a discussion of their differential needs and access to services.

6 I would refer the reader to the many innovative programs designed to address the whole spectrum of homelessness – not just chronic homelessness – that Gerald Daly (1996) documents in his book, *Homeless: Policies, Strategies and Lives on the Street* (see Chapter 11 in particular). He delineates a broad range of approaches throughout the United States, Great Britain, and Canada – including, information and advocacy centres, education projects, training programs, health projects and substance abuse programs, transitional housing, supportive housing, permanent housing, home-based support programs, cooperative housing, and self-help housing.

Chapter 4: Safe Haven

1 A yellowed, dog-eared 8½″ x 14″ typed sheet of paper with Marge Piercy's poem, 'Report of the Fourteenth Subcommittee on Convening a Discussion Group,' was taped to the wall of the room where many of the Resource Group meetings were held – close by the coffee machine.

2 Both Culhane's (1993) and Lipton's (1993) articles were part of an orientation manual, *Developing and Operating Safe Havens Programs* for a workshop sponsored by the Center for Mental Services, Substance Abuse and Mental Health Services Administration, U.S. Department of Health and Human Services, Office of Special Needs Assistance Programs, Office of Community Planning and Development and U.S. Department of Housing and Urban Development, April 1997, in Washington, DC. The workshop was intended to give technical assistance to agencies developing safe havens, and was designed to help develop a tool kit on developing and operating safe havens.

3 The joke about Mary-Jane having many names bears on one of the survival strategies that women living on the street may adopt. They use several names – to avoid detection by authorities, to access services, or to take on different roles.

4 The 'pinks' are pink-coloured forms that have to be signed by shelter users, in order for the shelters to obtain their per diem funding from Hostel Services. In other municipal facilities, it is standard practice to deny shelter to anyone who will not sign the forms.

Chapter 6: Come Inside

1 'Harm reduction' is a controversial approach advocated by many service providers and researchers working in the addictions field. Rather than working towards total abstinence when working with people with severe substance addictions, advocates concentrate on minimizing the dangers associated with use. The model accepts that total abstinence is unrealistic for many, and some harm may be inevitable (Emanuel and Suttor 1998:41).

Chapter 7: Natural Progression

1 Houselink's mission is to improve the quality of life of psychiatric survivors, homeless people, and others who have been marginalized by providing permanent, affordable, supportive housing.

Chapter 8: Long Road from the Street

1 Another study conducted for the government of British Columbia compares the cost of government services for homeless people with the cost of services for a person moving off the street to a permanent address (for example, government-supported housing). This study also concludes that government spending is significantly less for those who move from the streets to housing. 'Supportive housing is an effective option for individuals who may have been chronically homeless and who have the greatest difficulty in obtaining and maintaining housing' (British Columbia Ministry of Social Development and Economic Security 2001:3).

References

Abu-Lughod, Lila. 1991. Writing against culture. In *Recapturing Anthropology: Working in the Present*, ed. Richard G. Fox. Pp. 137–62. Santa Fe, NM: School of American Research Press.

Anderson, Rae (Rae Bridgman). 1997. Street as metaphor in housing for the homeless. *Journal of Social Distress and Homelessness* 6(1):1–12.

Aviram, U. 1990. Community care of the seriously mentally ill: continuing problems and current issues. *Community Mental Health Journal* 26(1):69–88.

Barrow, Sue M., Fredrick Hellman, Anne M. Lovell, Jane Plapinger, and Elmer L. Struening. 1992. Evaluating outreach services: lessons from five programs. *New Directions in Mental Health Services* 52:29–45.

Bassuk, E.L., J.C. Buckner, L.F. Weinreb, S.S. Browne, R. Dawson, and J.N. Perloff. 1997. Homelessness in female-headed families: childhood and adult risk and protective factors. *American Journal of Public Health* 87(2):249–55.

Baxter, E., and Kim Hopper. 1981 *Private Lives / Public Spaces: Homeless Adults on the Streets of New York City*. New York: Community Services Society.

Benson, Paul (ed.). 1993. *Anthropology and Literature*. Urbana: University of Illinois Press.

Boydell, Katherine, Brenda Gladstone, and Pam Roberts. 1999. *Savard's: A Descriptive Analysis*. (A Report submitted to Homes First.) Toronto: Community Support and Research Unit, Queen Street Mental Health Centre.

Bradshaw, Frances. 1984. Working with women. In *Making Space: Women and the Man-Made Environment*, ed. Matrix. Pp. 89–105. London: Pluto Press.

Breton, Margot. 1989. The need for mutual-aid groups in a drop-in for homeless women: the Sistering case. *Social Work with Groups* 11(4):47–61.

– 1984. A drop-in for transient women: using the physical environment to promote competence. *Social Work* 29(6):542–5.

Brettell, Caroline B. (ed.). 1996. *When They Read What We Write: The Politics of Ethnography.* Westport, CT: Bergin and Garvey.

Bridgman, Rae (Rae Anderson). 2002a. Fieldnotes from 'home': ethnography on exhibition. In *Design and the Social Sciences: Making Connections*, ed. Jorge Frascara. Pp. 125–134. London and New York: Taylor and Francis.

– 2002b. Housing chronically homeless women: 'inside' a safe haven. *Housing Policy Debate* 13(1):51–81.

– 2001a. Despite a forsaken and sacred trust: life in a safe haven for chronically homeless women. *International Journal of Mental Health* 30(2):79–89.

– 2001b. Testimony of a once homeless Aboriginal woman: I can only start from my own story. In *Pushing the Margins: Native and Northern Studies*, ed. Jill Oakes, Rick Riewe, and Skip Koolage. Pp. 322–37. Winnipeg: Departments of Native Studies and Zoology; and Faculty of Graduate Studies, University of Manitoba.

– 2000. My journey home: homeless and aboriginal and a woman. In *Aboriginal Health, Identity and Resources*, ed. Jill Oakes, Rick Riewe, Skip Koolage, Leanne Simpson, and Nancy Shuster. Pp. 93–104. Winnipeg, Departments of Native Studies and Zoology; and Faculty of Graduate Studies, University of Manitoba.

– 1999a. Fieldnotes from 'home': anthropology and design on exhibition. Paper presented at the annual meeting of the Canadian Anthropology Society / Société canadienne d'anthropologie, Université Laval, Québec, 15 May, and subsequently presented at the Design and Social Sciences Conference, University of Alberta, Edmonton, 1 Oct. 1999.

– 1999b. The street gives and the street takes: the meaning of the 'street' for those who are homeless. In *Therapeutic Landscapes: The Dynamic between Place and Wellness*, ed. Allison Williams. Pp. 153–66. Lanham, MD: University Press of America.

– 1999c. More than mere shelter: incorporating art in housing for the homeless. In *Common Ground: Contemporary Craft, Architecture and the Decorative Arts*, ed. Gloria Hickey. Ottawa: Institute for Contemporary Canadian Craft and the Canadian Museum of Civilization.

– 1999d. 'Oh, so you have a home to go to?': Empowerment and resistance in work with chronically homeless women. In *Feminist Fields: Ethnographic Insights*, ed. Rae Bridgman, Sally Cole, and Heather Howard-Bobiwash. Pp. 103–16. Peterborough, ON: Broadview Press.

– 1999e. House/Home. Exhibition of Strachan House architectural drawings, photographs and fieldnotes by Robert Burley and Debra Friedman, Janna Levitt and Dean Goodman, and Rae Bridgman. Photo Passage, Harbourfront Centre, Toronto, May to June.

– 1998a. A 'city' within the city: a Canadian housing model for the homeless. *Open House International* 23(1):12–21.

– 1998b. The architecture of homelessness and utopian pragmatics. *Utopian Studies* 9(1):50–67.

Bridgman, Rae, Sally Cole, and Heather Howard-Bobiwash. 1999. *Feminist Fields: Ethnographic Insights*. Peterborough, ON: Broadview Press.

British Columbia, Ministry of Social Development and Economic Security. 2001. *Homelessness – Causes and Effects: The Relationship between Homelessness and the Health, Social Services and Criminal Justice Systems*. (A Review of the Literature.) Victoria: The Ministry of Social Development and Economic Security.

Brookman, Ann, and Sandra Morgen. 1988. *Women and the Politics of Empowerment*. Philadelphia: Temple University Press.

Brown, Kaaren Strauch, and Marjorie Ziefert. 1990. A feminist approach to working with homeless women. *Affilia: Journal of Women and Social Work* 5(1):7–26.

Burt, Martha R. 1992. *Over the Edge: The Growth of Homelessness in the 1980s*. New York: Russell Sage Foundation; Washington, DC: Urban Institute Press.

Butler, Sandra S. 1994. *Middle-Aged, Female and Homeless: The Stories of a Forgotten Group*. New York: Garland.

Canada Mortgage and Housing Corporation (CMHC). 1999a. National Roundtable on Best Practices Addressing Homelessness. Ottawa, 14–15 June.

– 1999b. *Best Practices for Alleviating Homelessness*. (Report, Distinct Housing Needs Series.) Ottawa: CMHC.

Cohen, Neal L. 1992. Psychiatric outreach to the mentally ill. *New Directions in Mental Health Services* 52:29–45.

Cole, Sally. 1992. Anthropological lives: the reflexive tradition in a social science. In *Essays in Life Writing: From Genre to Critical Practice*, ed. Marlene Kadar. Pp. 113–27. Toronto: University of Toronto Press.

Cole, Sally, and Lynne Phillips. 1995. *Ethnographic Feminisms: Essays in Anthropology*. Ottawa: Carleton University Press.

Corbett, Tom. 2000. Process evaluations and the next generation of welfare reform. Paper presented at the National Academy of Sciences Workshop. Panel on Data and Methods for Measuring the Effects of Changes in Social Welfare Programs. Washington, DC, 4–5 Feb.

Culhane, Dennis. 1997. Testimony of Dennis P. Culhane, PhD, University of Pennsylvania. U.S. House of Representatives, Committee on Banking and Financial Services, Subcommittee on Housing and Community Opportunity. H.R. 217, Homeless Housing Programs Consolidation and Flexibility Act. (5 March).

– 1992. Ending homelessness among women with severe mental illness: a model program from Philadelphia. *Psychosocial Rehabilitation Journal* 16(1):73–6.

Daly, Gerald. 1996. *Homeless: Policies, Strategies, and Lives on the Street*. New York: Routledge.

Darnell, Regna. 1999. Winners announced for Turner Prize. *Anthropology News* 40(8):29–30.

D'Ercole, Ann, and Elmer Struening. 1990. Victimization among homeless women: implications for service delivery. *Journal of Community Psychology* 18:141–52.

Desjarlais, Robert. 1997. *Shelter Blues: Sanity and Selfhood among the Homeless*. Philadelphia: University of Pennsylvania Press.

Emmanuel, Barbara, and Greg Suttor. 1998. *Background Paper for the Homelessness Action Task Force*. Report prepared for Dr Anne Golden, President, United Way of Greater Toronto.

Erickson, Ken. 1990. New immigrants and the social service agency: changing relations at SRS. *Urban Anthropology* 19(4):387–407.

Evans, Patricia M., and Gerda R. Wekerle. 1997. *Women and the Canadian Welfare State: Challenges and Change*. Toronto: University of Toronto Press.

Farge, Brenda Doyle. 1989. Homeless women and freedom of choice. *Canadian Journal of Community Mental Health* 8(1):135–45.

– 1988. Hostels for Single Women: Subjectivity, Discourse and Social Regulation. Unpublished PhD dissertation, University of Toronto.

Foucault, Michel. 1975. *The Birth of the Clinic: An Archaeology of Medical Perception*. (Translated by A.M. Sheridan Smith.) New York: Vintage.

Gardiner, Michael. 1995. Utopia and everyday life in French social thought. *Utopian Studies* 6(2):90–123.

Glasser, Irene. 1994. *Homelessness in Global Perspective*. New York: G.K. Hall and Company.

Glasser, Irene, and Rae Bridgman. 1999. *Braving the Street: The Anthropology of Homelessness*. New York: Berghahn Books.

Goffman, Erving. 1961. *Asylums: Essays on the Social Situation of Mental Patients and Other Inmates*. Chicago: Aldine.

Golden, Anne, William Currie, Elizabeth Greaves, and E. John Atimer. 1999. *Taking Responsibility for Homelessness: An Action Plan for Toronto*. Toronto: City of Toronto Mayor's Homelessness Action Task Force.

Goldsack, Laura. 1999. A haven in a heartless world? Women and domestic violence. In *Ideal Homes? Social Change and Domestic Life*, ed. Tony Chapman and Jenny Hockey. Pp. 121–32. New York: Routledge.

Grenier, Paola. 1996. *Still Dying for a Home: An Update of Crisis' 1992 Investigation into the Links between Homelessness, Health and Mortality*. (Report.) London: Crisis.

Harman, Lesley D. 1989. *When a Hostel Becomes a Home*. Toronto: Garamond.

Harris, Maxine. 1991. *Sisters of the Shadow*. Norman: University of Oklahoma Press.

Herman, D.G., E.S. Susser, E.L. Struening, and B. Link. 1997. Adverse childhood experiences: are they risk factors for adult homelessness? *American Journal of Public Health* 87(2):249–55.

Holston, James. 1989. *The Modernist City: An Anthropological Critique of Brasilia*. Chicago: University of Chicago Press.

Hulchanski, David. 2000. A New Canadian Pastime? Counting Homeless People: Addressing and Preventing 'Homelessness' Is a Political Problem, Not a Statistical or Definitional Problem. Available online <http://resources.web.net/show.cfm?id=977&APP=housing>

Johnson, Laura C., and Allison Ruddock (Canadian Housing and Renewal Association). 2000. *Building Capacity: Enhancing Women's Economic Participation through Housing*. (Policy Research Report.) Ottawa: Status of Women Canada. Also available online <http://www.swc.cfc.gc.ca/>

Kiesler, C.A. 1991. Homelessness and public policy priorities. *American Psychologist* 46(1):1245–52.

Koegel, Paul. 1988. *Understanding Homelessness: An Ethnographic Approach*. Los Angeles: Los Angeles Homelessness Project.

Koegel, Paul, E. Melamid, and A. Berman. 1995. Childhood risk factors for homelessness among homeless adults. *American Journal of Public Health* 85(2):1642–9.

Kuhn, Randall, and Dennis Culhane. 1998. Applying cluster analysis to test a typology of homelessness by pattern of shelter utilization: results from the analysis of administrative data. *American Journal of Community Psychology* 26(2):201–32.

Kushner, Carol. 1998. *Better Access, Better Care: A Research Paper on Health Services and Homelessness in Toronto*. Report prepared for the City of Toronto Mayor's Homelessness Task Force.

Lamphere, Louise. (ed.). 1992. *Structuring Diversity: Ethnographic Perspectives on the New Immigration*. Chicago: University of Chicago Press.

Landsberg, Michele. 1997. Where will homeless women go if new shelter dies? *Toronto Star*, 8 June 1997, p. 2.

Layton, Jack. 2000. *Homelessness: The Making and Unmaking of a Crisis*. Toronto: Penguin Books / McGill Institute.

Liddiard, Mark, and Susan Hutson. 1991. Homeless young people and runaways: agency definitions and processes. *Journal of Social Policy* 20:365–88.

Liebow, Elliot. 1993. *Tell Them Who I Am: The Lives of Homeless Women*. New York: Free Press.

Lindsay, Sheryl. 1993. *Notes from visit to 'Women of Hope,' Philadelphia, April 1993*. Report, Women Street Survivors Project Orientation Manual (Jan. 1997).

Lionnet, F. 1995. Logiques metisses: cultural appropriation and postcolonial representations. In *Postcolonial Representations: Women, Literature and Identity*. Pp. 1–21. Ithaca, NY: Cornell University Press.

Lipton, Frank R. 1993. Housing homeless people with severe mental illness: why safe havens? Paper presented at 'Creating Safe Havens for Homeless Persons with Severe Mental Illness,' a workshop sponsored by the Center for Mental Health Services, Substance Abuse and Mental Health Services Administration, U.S. Department of Health and Human Services; and the U.S. Department of Housing and Urban Development, Washington, DC, 18–19 Nov.

Lovell, Anne M. 1997. 'The city is my mother': narratives of schizophrenia and homelessness. *American Anthropologist* 99(2):355–68.

– 1984. Marginality with isolation: social networks and the new homeless. Paper presented at the 83rd Annual Meeting of the American Anthropological Association, Denver, Colorado, 14–18 November.

Lovell, Anne M., and Sandra Cohn. 1998. The elaboration of 'choice' in a program for homeless persons labeled psychiatrically disabled. *Human Organization* 57(1):8–20.

Low, Nicholas, and Bruce Crawshaw. 1985. Homeless youth: patterns of belief. *Australian Journal of Social Issues* 20(1):23–34.

Lyon-Callo, Vincent. 1998. Constraining responses to homelessness: an ethnographic exploration of the impact of funding concerns on resistance. *Human Organization* 47(1):1–7.

Mayor's Homelessness Task Force. 1999. *Taking Responsibility for Homelessness: An Action Plan for Toronto*. Toronto.

Mental Health Policy Research Group. 1998. *Mental Illness and Pathways into Homelessness: Findings and Implications*. Report prepared for the City of Toronto Mayor's Homelessness Action Task Force.

Mercier, Céline, and Guylaine Racine. 1995. Case management with homeless women: a descriptive study. *Community Mental Health Journal* 31(1):25–37.

Metropolitan Toronto District Health Council. 1996. *Metropolitan Toronto Mental Health Reform*. Final Report, Dec. System Design and Implementation Recommendations.

Montgomery, C. 1994. Swimming upstream: the strengths of women who survive homelessness. *Advances in Nursing Science* 16(3):34–45.

Mowbray, Carol T., Evan Cohen, and Deborah Bybee. 1991. Services to individuals who are homeless and mentally ill: implementation evaluation. In *Eval-*

uating Programs for the Homeless (New Directions for Program Evaluation, vol. 52), ed. Debra J. Rog. Pp. 75–90. San Francisco: Jossey-Bass.

Myers, Mary Anne S. 1997. Invisible populations of the poor: professional perspectives and service system outcasts. Paper presented at the American Anthropology Association Annual Meeting, Washington, DC, 20 Nov.

Novac, Sylvia. (1995). Seeking shelter: feminist home truths. In *Change of Plans: Towards a Non-Sexist Sustainable City,* ed. Margrit Eichler. Pp. 51–70. Toronto: Garamond.

Novac, Sylvia, Joyce Brown, and Carmen Bourbonnais. 1996. *No Room of Her Own: A Literature Review on Women and Homelessness.* (Research Report.) Ottawa: CMHC.

Novac, Sylvia, Joyce Brown, and Gloria Gallant. 1999. *Women on the Rough Edge: A Decade of Change for Long-Term Homeless Women.* (Research Report.) Ottawa: CMHC.

Novac, Sylvia, Joyce Brown, Gloria Gallant, and Vicki Sanders. 1998. *New Directions and Options for Habitat Services.* (Report.) Toronto: Community Mental Health Program.

Novac, Sylvia, Joyce Brown, Alison Guyton, and Mary Ann Quance. 1996. *Borderlands of Homelessness: Women's Views on Alternative Housing.* (Research Report.) Toronto: The Women's Services Network.

Novac, Sylvia, and Mary Ann Quance. 1998. *Back to Community: An Assessment of Supportive Housing in Toronto.* Report prepared for the City of Toronto Mayor's Homelessness Action Task Force.

Obonsawin-Irwin Consulting. 1998. *A Planning Framework for Addressing Aboriginal Homelessness in the City of Toronto.* Report prepared for the City of Toronto Mayor's Homelessness Action Task Force.

Ontario Provincial Task Force on Homelessness. 1998. *Report of the Ontario Provincial Task Force on Homelessness.* Ottawa.

O'Reilly-Fleming, T. 1993. *Down and Out in Canada: Homeless Canadians.* Toronto: Canadian Scholars' Press.

Peressini, Tracy L. Lynne McDonald, and David Hulchanski. 1996. *Estimating Homelessness: Towards a Methodology for Counting the Homeless in Canada.* Background Report prepared for Social and Economic Policy and Research Division. Ottawa: CMHC.

Pirie, Marion. 1998. From center to margin and back again: defending mental health programs for women in Ontario. *International Journal of Mental Health* 27(2):72–84.

Pomeroy, Steve, and Will Dunning. 1998. *Housing Solutions to Homelessness: Cost-Benefit Analysis of Different Types of Shelter. Preliminary Assessment.* (Final Report.) City of Toronto. Mayor's Homelessness Action Task Force.

Racine, Guylaine. 1993. L'intervention en santé mentale: le mandat inattendu des maisons d'hébergement pour femmes sans abri. *Santé mentale au Québec* 18(1):251–68.

Reimer, Frances. 1997. From welfare to working poor: prioritizing practice in research on employment-training programs for the poor. *Anthropology and Education Quarterly* 28(1):85–110.

Rendell, Jane, Barbara Penner, and Iain Borden (eds.). 2000. *Gender Space Architecture: An Interdisciplinary Introduction*. New York: Routledge.

Ritchey, Ferris, J. La Gory, and Jeffry Mullis. 1991. Gender differences in health risks and physical symptoms among the homeless. *Journal of Health and Social Behavior* 32: 33–48.

Rochefort, David A. 1997. *From Poorhouses to Homelessness: Policy Analysis and Mental Health*, 2nd ed. Westport, CT: Auburn House.

Rosenthal, Rob. 1991. Straighter from the source: alternative methods of researching homelessness. *Urban Anthropology* 20(2):109–26.

Ross, Aileen. 1982. *The Lost and the Lonely: Homeless Women in Montreal*. Montreal: Canadian Human Rights Foundation.

Rossi, P.H., J.D. Wright, B.A. Fisher, and G. Willis. 1987. The urban homeless: estimating composition and size. *Science* (March): 1336–41.

Sachs, Patricia. (ed.) 1989. Anthropological Approaches to Organizational Culture. (Theme issue.) *Anthropology of Work Review* 10(3).

Sandercock, Leonie. 1995. Voices from the borderlands: a meditation on a metaphor. *Journal of Planning Education and Research* 14: 77–88.

Schneekloth, Lynda. 1994. Partial utopian visions: feminist reflections from the field. In *Women and the Environment*, ed. Irwin Altman and Arza Churchman. Pp. 281–306. New York: Plenum.

Schaer, Roland, Gregory Claeys, and Lyman Tower Sargent. 2000. *Utopia: The Search for the Ideal Society in the Western World*. New York: New York Public Library / Oxford University Press.

Schneider, Jo Anne. 2001. Introduction: social welfare and welfare reform. *American Anthropologist* 103(3):705–13.

Segal, S., and J. Baumohl. 1985. The community living-room. *Social Casework* (Feb.):111–16.

Smith, Elizabeth M., and Carol S. North. 1994. Not all homeless women are alike: effects of motherhood and the presence of children. *Community Mental Health Journal* 30(6):601–10.

Sohng, Sung Sil Lee. 1996. Supported housing for the mentally ill elderly: implementation and consumer choice. *Community Mental Health Journal* 32: 135–48.

Springer, Joe, James Mars, and Melissa Dennison. 1998. *A Profile of the Toronto Homeless Population*. Report prepared for the City of Toronto Mayor's Homelessness Action Task Force.

SPR Associates, Inc. 1998. *Canadian Women and Their Housing: 1997*. (Research Report.) Ottawa: CMHC.

Susser, Ezra, Stephen M. Goldfinger, and Andrea White. 1990. Some clinical approaches to the homeless mentally ill. *Community Mental Health Journal* 26:463–80.

Thrasher, S.P., and Mowbray, C.T. 1995. A strengths perspective: an ethnographic study of homeless women with children. *Health and Social Work* 20(2):93–101.

Tomas, Annabel, and Helga Dittmar. 1995. The experience of homeless women: an exploration of housing histories and the meaning of home. *Housing Studies* 10(4):493–515.

Torrey, E. Fuller. 1990. Economic barriers to widespread implementation of model programs for the seriously mentally ill. *Hospital and Community Psychiatry* 41(5):526–31.

United Nations Human Rights Committee. 1999. *International Covenant on Civil and Political Rights*. Consideration of Reports submitted by States Parties under Article 40 of the Covenant. New York: United Nations.

Ward, Jim (Associates). 1998a. *Locally Based Approaches to Prevention and Rescue from Homelessness*. Report prepared for the City of Toronto Mayor's Homelessness Action Task Force.

– 1998b. *The Role and Function of Emergency Hostels in Dealing with Homelessness*. Report prepared for the City of Toronto Mayor's Homelessness Action Task Force.

Ward, Jim (Associates), and Jacques Tremblay. 1998. *Homeless Voices: Follow-up to Homeless, Not Helpless*. (Report.) Toronto: Healthy City Office.

Watson, Sophie, with Helen Austerberry. 1986. *Housing and Homelessness: A Feminist Perspective*. London: Routledge and Kegan Paul.

Wekerle, Gerda R. 1993. Responding to diversity: housing developed by and for women. *Canadian Journal of Urban Research* 2(2):95–113.

Wekerle, Gerda R., and Sylvia Novac. (1989). Developing two women's housing cooperatives. In *New Households, New Housing*, ed. Karen Franck and Sherry Ahrentzen. Pp. 223–43. New York: Van Nostrand Reinhold.

Williams, Jean Calterone. 1996. Geography of the homeless shelter: staff surveillance and resident resistance. *Urban Anthropology* 25:75–113.

Wolch, Jennifer, and Michael Dear. 1993. *Malign Neglect: Homelessness in an American City*. San Francisco: Jossey-Bass.

Wolf, Margery. 1992. *A Thrice-Told Tale: Feminism, Postermodernism, and Ethno-graphic Responsibility.* Stanford: Stanford University Press.

Women Street Survivors Resource Group. 1996. *The Women Street Survivors Project: Programme Description and First Principles.* Toronto: Women Street Survivors Resource Group.

Wright, Susan. 1994. *The Anthropology of Organizations.* New York: Routledge.

Yamashita, Bob. 1995. The Philadelphia experiment. *Inside Storeys* (newsletter, spring edition). Toronto: City of Toronto Housing Department and City-home.

Index